W9-DCW-242

Tales from the Mets Dugout

Bruce Markusen

SP
SPORTS
PUBLISHING
L.L.C.

www.SportsPublishingLLC.com

ISBN: 1-58261-983-2

Publishers: Peter L. Bannon and Joseph J. Bannon Sr.
Senior managing editor: Susan M. Moyer
Acquisitions editor: Mike Pearson
Developmental editor: Regina D. Sabbia
Art director: K. Jeffrey Higgerson
Book design: Joseph Brumleve
Dust jacket design: Dustin Hubbart
Project manager: Kathryn R. Holleman
Imaging: Heidi Norsen and K. Jeffrey Higgerson
Photo editor: Erin Linden-Levy
Vice president of sales and marketing: Kevin King
Media and promotions managers: Courtney Hainline (regional),
     Randy Fouts (national), Maurey Williamson (print)

Printed in the United States of America

Sports Publishing L.L.C.
804 North Neil Street
Champaign, IL 61820

Phone: 1-877-424-2665
Fax: 217-363-2073
Web site: www.SportsPublishingLLC.com

This book is dedicated to the memory of my father, Stanley G. Markusen, a Mets fan from the beginning. If not for him, I never would have written this baseball book, or any other.

Contents

Acknowledgments

Many generous people have offered their time and efforts in contributing to *Tales from the Mets Dugout*.

I'd like to offer special thanks to baseball writer and researcher Maxwell Kates, who offered helpful suggestions, contributed story ideas and material, and graciously made available interview transcripts with former Mets players Rod Gaspar and Ron Taylor.

Thanks also to Wanda Chirnside for filming and producing the interview with Ron Taylor, and to Ron "Metsie" Bleiberg for story contribution.

Thanks to the following players, coaches, broadcasters, and wives for providing interview material for the book: Gary Carter, Gary Cohen, Pam Frisella, Rod Gaspar, Elliott Maddox, Bill Monbouquette, Howie Rose, Tom Seaver, and Ron Taylor. Thanks to internet baseball historians Darren "Repoz" Viola and Steve Treder for their insightful story contributions. Thanks also to prolific baseball author Dan Schlossberg for his help in arranging interviews.

As usual, a baseball book detailing the game's history could not be written without the assistance of the fine staff at the National Baseball Hall of Fame Library in Cooperstown, New York. Thanks to Freddy Berowski, Claudette Burke, Bill Francis, Jeremy Jones, Gabriel Schechter, Tim Wiles, and Russell Wolinsky. Thanks also to Hall of Fame staffers Jeff Arnett and Amanda Pinney.

Finally, thanks to lifelong Mets fan and publishing expert Matt Silverman for his careful reading and examination of the manuscript.

CHAPTER ONE

The Early Years

Inauspicious Beginnings

I t's commonly known that the Mets lost their first game in franchise history, setting the stage for a nine-game losing streak that would put Casey Stengel's motley crew in an early-season hole from which it would never recover. Yet, not quite as well publicized is the unlucky happenstance that befell a number of Mets players earlier in the day as they awaited the arrival of Game 1. With the team preparing to play the St. Louis Cardinals at Busch Stadium, the players, coaches, and manager all spent the previous evening at the Chase Hotel in downtown St. Louis. On the morning of the franchise opener, players piled into the elevator cars at the hotel on their way to meet the team bus. Thanks to an elevator malfunction, 16 of the players found themselves stuck at the hotel for an extra 20 minutes, making them late for pregame workouts.

The Mets' debut soon turned into a disaster, as Stengel's troops fell to the Cardinals, 11-4. They would have been better off stuck in the elevators at the Chase Hotel. That way, the Mets could have taken a 9-0 forfeit loss and avoided the pain and embarrassment they endured in being blown out by the rival Redbirds.

The Pitcher and the Pickoff

Roger Craig is best remembered for two things: his ability to teach pitchers the split-fingered fastball during a successful reign as manager of the San Francisco Giants, and for losing a ton of games while pitching for the Mets toward the end of his career.

As a pitcher, Craig had a habit that also became well known—and occasionally annoyed opposing players. He liked to throw over to first base frequently, sometimes to the level of obsession. A point in case happened during the Mets' inaugural season.

On a hot afternoon, the Mets played the Milwaukee Braves. A runner reached base for the Braves, bringing left-handed slugger Eddie Mathews to the plate. During the course of Mathews's at-bat, Craig threw over to first base *14* times, which might have become some sort of unofficial record. The repeated pickoff attempts became so disconcerting to Mathews that he shouted at Craig and complained to the home plate umpire. With sweat dripping on his face and arms, Mathews took a break, walked over to the dugout, and wiped himself off with a towel. Mathews then returned to the plate, where he preceded to strike out against a stubborn—but successful—Craig.

A Rematch of Old-Timers

File this one in the category of "not making sense."

Now that the Mets have established over 40 years of history as a National League franchise, they no longer stage an annual "Old-Timers Day" exhibition. Yet, in their first year of existence, with no history to speak of, they held their first ever Old-Timers Game. With no "past" Mets to call their own, the Mets honored the roots of National League baseball in New York City by inviting former members of the Brooklyn Dodgers and New York Giants to participate in a day of ceremony and exhibition baseball on July 14, 1962.

The Mets also showed a penchant for theatrics by setting up an intriguing matchup between two retired players, one a former Dodgers pitcher and the other a onetime Giants slugger. Ex-Dodger Ralph Branca faced former Giant Bobby Thomson 11 years after their famed meeting in the historic National League playoff game at the Polo Grounds.

On that memorable fall day in 1951, Thomson had lifted a fly-ball home run to left field against Branca, giving the Giants their most dramatic National League pennant ever. This time around, with the Polo Grounds once again providing the setting, Branca fared much better. He retired Thomson on a routine fly ball to center field. Not too many baseball fans remembered the "second" meeting between Branca and Thomson, but for those who attended the first Mets Old-Timers Day at the Polo Grounds, they received a fond memory from a new franchise that seemed to care about New York's rich baseball history.

A Swansong of a Triple Play

In a year in which they lost a record 120 games, it was especially fitting that the Mets lost their last game of the season and also suffered the ultimate of offensive embarrassments—a triple play.

In the eighth inning of a 5-1 loss to the Chicago Cubs at Wrigley Field, the Mets placed their first two runners on base. Mets catcher Joe Pignatano, a future staple of the organization as a coach, then lofted a fly ball into short right field, which rookie second baseman Ken Hubbs snared by making a fine running catch. Noticing that Mets outfielder Richie Ashburn had strayed too far off first base, Hubbs threw the ball back toward Ernie Banks for the inning's second out. Banks then fired the ball to second base, where Mets infielder Sammy Drake had also misjudged the fly ball and had already made his way to third base. Cubs shortstop Andre Rodgers touched the bag for the third out, completing the rarest of defensive plays.

By a bizarre coincidence, the triple play represented the major league swansong for the three Mets participants—Pignatano, Ashburn, and Drake. None of them ever again played in a major league game.

Elio Chacon

Richie Ashburn's retirement after the Mets' inaugural season left the fledgling team with a major hole in center field. At a press conference held in February of 1963 at 680 Fifth Avenue in New York City, a reporter asked manager Casey Stengel how he planned to replace Ashburn.

"Elio Chacon?" Stengel asked rhetorically in referring to a young man who had played shortstop, but had virtually no major league experience as an outfielder. "Where could I play him regularly? He can run and throw, but his shortstop is too deep and his RBIs too few."

As he offered his not-so-enthusiastic endorsement, none of the writers dared to ask Stengel what he meant by his "shortstop is too deep," but they certainly understood the part about the "RBIs being too few." About a month later, Chacon himself was asked about the possibility of playing center field.

"What's a matter, I no play good short last year?" said Chacon, a native of Venezuela who was phonetically quoted with improper use of grammar by an insensitive reporter. "But Casey is boss and if he say play outfield, I try."

Well, Chacon gave it a try, went 0-for-17, and earned an early demotion to Triple-A Buffalo. There he resumed playing, presumably with his "shortstop too deep."

Choo Choo

Casey Stengel didn't have much real talent at his disposal during his days as the first Mets manager, but then again, he didn't always have the keenest eye for evaluating his talent. A prime example was young catcher-outfielder Clarence "Choo Choo" Coleman, whom Casey raved about during the spring of 1963.

"About this Choo Coleman," Casey told Dan Daniel of *The Sporting News*, sounding like a lawyer addressing a jury in court. "Is he a catcher or an outfielder? I will find out at St. Petersburg [the Mets' spring training home in Florida]. I say he is the sleeper of the roster. Watch this carefully."

The Mets and their fans watched carefully, but they didn't like what they saw. As a catcher, Coleman couldn't field or throw—and he couldn't hit either. In 1963, he finished the season with more errors (15) than RBIs (nine), which is hard to do for a catcher. Regarded by some as one of the worst players in the history of the franchise, Coleman became best known for snapping at Ralph Kiner after an innocent question on the broadcaster's trademark *Kiner's Korner* postgame show.

When Kiner asked Coleman what his wife's name was and "What's she like?" Coleman replied rather caustically: "Her name's Mrs. Coleman, and she likes me." With that remark, Coleman reached the highlight of his career in a Mets uniform.

One Chunky Hombre

Casey Stengel wasn't the only member of the Mets' brass guilty of overestimating the value of his players. Toward the tail end of the 1962 season, the Mets made a transaction with the Boston Red Sox, acquiring pitcher Galen Cisco, whom one writer for *The Sporting News* described as a "chunky hombre." At five feet, 11 inches and 215 pounds, Cisco certainly looked to be on the ample side, but the Mets liked his arm far more than his physique, or his poor statistics (a 4-7 record with a voluminous 6.72 ERA for the Red Sox in 1962). During the winter, the Mets' front office made some bold predictions about Cisco.

"Cisco is quite likely to show up as one of our starting pitchers," Mets president (and de facto general manager) George Weiss told *The Sporting News* in January. Weiss's optimistic assessment of Cisco prompted a doubting response from one writer.

"I am quite willing to accept your estimate of this pitcher's value," said the writer, "but frankly I am puzzled."

Weiss hesitated little in reinforcing his claim.

"Just keep an eye on Cisco," Weiss said confidently. "Johnny Murphy [the Mets' chief scout and administrative assistant] says not to worry about his Boston record."

Hall of Famer Casey Stengel exhibits the frustration of early Mets ineptitude. National Baseball Hall of Fame Library/MLB Photos/Getty Images

Mets fans soon started to worry. In 1963, Cisco would post a won-loss record of 7-15 with a bulky ERA of 4.34 (a high ERA during an era dominated by pitchers), while making only 17 starts. So much for lofty predictions.

The First Good Catcher

Where Choo Choo Coleman failed, Jesse Gonder succeeded. Although mostly a journeyman catcher throughout his career, Gonder played his finest seasons in 1963 and 1964 as a member of the Mets. After starting the 1963 season with the Cincinnati Reds, Gonder found himself traded to the Mets in mid-stream. He responded to the move by hitting .302 in 126 at-bats. In 1964, he compiled a respectable .270 batting average in 131 games while giving New York some much-desired respectability beyond the plate. Gonder, who passed away in 2004 at the age of 68, also gained notoriety for other reasons. Having debuted with the cross-town "Bronx Bombers" in 1960, Gonder became one of the first players to play for both the Yankees and the Mets during his major league career.

More importantly, Gonder established a reputation for being outspoken and honest at a time when most African-American athletes found little encouragement—and numerous obstacles—in doing so. Shortly after his death, Gonder's daughter, Tanya, praised him for his courage in being willing to tell the truth.

"Daddy was extremely outspoken, and when he played baseball, that wasn't very popular," his daughter told the *Oakland Tribune*. "He was honest and competitive, a straight shooter. You knew where you stood with him."

For some reason, Gonder never recaptured his success of 1963 and 1964. The Mets, who liked his left-handed swing and envisioned him as their catcher for the foreseeable future, watched him regress the following season, which prompted the organization to deal him to the Milwaukee Braves in mid-season.

After his playing days, Gonder became a bus driver for Golden Gate Transit in the Bay Area, remaining in that position for two decades. He then retired in the mid-1990s, promptly enjoying the benefits of life without work.

"After retirement it was all bowling and poker," his daughter said. "He was a very good father, a devoted family man." He certainly was a good man, one who carved out his own small, but memorable niche in the early history of the Mets' franchise.

Rotten Apples

Former Yankees outfielder Gene Woodling became the centerpiece of one of the Mets' earliest controversies, an episode that came to a head because of apples. Yes, apples. After playing the second half of the 1962 season with the Mets, Woodling pursued an opportunity to serve as a player-coach with the Yankees, but the Mets refused to relinquish their rights to the veteran outfielder. The Mets did, however, make Woodling a player-coach, giving him the same role that he would have had in the Bronx. So in the spring of 1963, a forgiving Woodling reported to the Mets' spring training site claiming that he was "not mad at anybody" over the organization's refusal to allow him to move to the crosstown Yankees.

On one of the early days of the spring, Woodling found himself in the clubhouse with teammate Marv "Marvelous Marv" Throneberry. Unhappy with his contract, Throneberry expressed his frustration to Woodling and told him that he wanted to talk to team president George Weiss about the situation but had been unable to do so.

"You certainly should [be allowed to talk to Weiss]," remarked Woodling. "You paid your own way down here."

By a stroke of bad luck, Weiss's top aide, Johnny Murphy, happened to hear Woodling's remark and immediately jumped to the defense of Weiss. Woodling then snapped back at Murphy, with a nasty shouting match ensuing in the clubhouse. When Weiss learned about the incident, he described it as "an intolerable mess."

On March 3, the Mets waived Woodling for the purpose of giving him his unconditional release. A defensive Weiss did his best to explain the situation. He claimed that Woodling was unhappy that the Mets had introduced him as only a player, and not as a player-coach, at the beginning of spring training. Weiss claimed it was a simple oversight, but some wondered why Casey Stengel hadn't been informed of Woodling's status right from the start. Woodling felt he had been put in an awkward situation.

And then there was the clinching controversy involving the apples, which Weiss strangely referred to as the "diet episode." After one spring practice, some players had apparently come into the clubhouse only to find that the traditional food spread had already been cleared. The players then asked for a few apples, but were told that they could not have any. Woodling then pointed out that there was a refrigerator in the next room full of apples, but his request was also rejected out of hand. Woodling's attempt to extract some apples for himself and his teammates was apparently the final straw, at least in the mind of the notoriously thrifty (and at times petty) George Weiss.

An Honest Assessment

Unlike most of today's managers, who avoid criticizing players at all costs and use politically correct language in assessing their teams' poor performances, Casey Stengel reveled in bluntness. After emerging as the No. 1 reliever on the Mets' 1962 team, Craig Anderson endured a terrible spring training in 1963, earning himself a surprising demotion to the minor leagues. Stengel offered little sympathy in assessing Anderson's poor spring and his sudden change of fortune.

"Let him pitch his way back," said an annoyed Stengel. "He had his full share of chances."

After a stint in the minor leagues, Anderson would pitch in only seven more games for the Mets—with disastrous results—before watching his major league career come to an unceremonious end.

Jim Hickman and Ed Sullivan

As poorly as the Mets played throughout much of the 1960s, one of their players once received an invitation to appear on the celebrated *Ed Sullivan Show*. Outfielder-third baseman Jim Hickman was scheduled to appear on the popular program on the evening of April 21, 1963. Since the show was aired live, Hickman had to arrive at the studio by no later than eight o'clock Eastern time; he would receive a nice bonus of $250 for making his appearance on the program.

As it turned out, the Mets had a doubleheader scheduled for that afternoon. Sure enough, the second game ran late, ending at 10 minutes after eight, and forced Hickman to miss his appearance on national television. To make matters worse, Hickman had to forfeit the $250 from the Sullivan people, which would have come in handy for a player in the years prior to arbitration and free agency.

Fear Strikes Out in New York

On May 23, 1963, the Mets acquired colorful journeyman Jimmy Piersall from the Washington Senators in a deal that was linked to the recent trade that allowed Gil Hodges to become the manager of the team in the Capitol City. (At the time, the Mets denied an association between the Piersall and Hodges trades, but later research showed the moves to be interlocked.)

At one time a top-flight young outfielder with the Boston Red Sox, Piersall also possessed a dark side. An emotionally charged outfielder who eventually became the subject of the film, *Fear Strikes Out*, Piersall often became a focal point of fan and media attention because of his offbeat behavior. Opinions within the baseball world were split on Piersall; some considered him merely colorful and clownish, while others believed he was emotionally disturbed and in need of counseling. Piersall didn't last long in Mets pinstripes, but he succeeded in making a memorable impression in New York.

When the Mets staged Old-Timers' Day on June 22, Piersall decided to keep himself busy by serving as the home plate umpire. During his tour of duty as a guest arbiter, Piersall kicked dirt on home plate and grabbed a catcher's mitt so that he could warm up one of the old-time pitchers. In perhaps his most celebrated move, Piersall decided to switch places with former Brooklyn Dodger Gene Hermanski in the batter's box, taking an exaggerated swing against one of the old-timer offerings. Piersall couldn't resist a bit of controversy either, as he decided to eject *fellow umpire* Charlie Berry for alleged incompetence.

While Piersall succeeded in amusing most observers with his Old-Timers Day antics, he didn't please his manager—or baseball's commissioner—the following day. Playing in a game at the Polo Grounds, Piersall clubbed his 100th career home run. To honor the occasion, Piersall decided to run the bases in a rather unconventional manner.

As he started for first base, Piersall turned his body around and proceeded to run the bases backwards. As he approached each base, he carefully turned his head to make sure that he touched each base, then continued with his backwards jaunt. Piersall's unusual home run trot angered three people in particular: Phillies pitcher Dallas Green, who surrendered the home run; Mets manager Casey Stengel, who felt all clowning should be restricted to the manager ("There's room for only one clown on this team," Stengel said famously.); and Commissioner Ford C. Frick, who warned Piersall never to do it again.

One month later, on July 22, the Mets released Piersall, ending his 60-day tenure with the team. Team executive and administrative assistant Johnny Murphy claimed that Piersall's antics had nothing to do with the decision, instead pointing to Piersall's miniscule batting average, but with the front office manned by the ever-conservative George Weiss, some Mets fans were left to wonder.

As for Stengel, he seemed to have mixed feelings about Piersall. On the one hand, he called Piersall the "greatest defensive outfielder" he had ever seen. On the other, he expressed doubts about Piersall's ability to perform well on the pressurized stage of the major leagues. "He's great," Stengel acknowledged, "but you gotta play him in a cage."

Cosell vs. Casey

Not all observers of the Mets in the early 1960s regarded Casey Stengel as cute and clownish. One of his most vocal critics could be found on the Mets' pregame and postgame radio shows. The critic would become better known in later years for his commentary on boxing matches and football broadcasts, but in 1963, he might have been regarded as Stengel's No. 1 nemesis.

"When the Mets win, it's because Casey told them how to do it. When they lose, it's because someone didn't do something right," complained Howard Cosell, who co-hosted the Mets' radio program with former Brooklyn Dodgers right-hander Ralph Branca.

Regarding Stengel as a self-promoter and finger-pointer, Cosell let loose with his typically sarcastic and abrasive analysis.

"The Mets have won 74 games and lost 190 in their [first] two years, so that means the manager has a record of 74-and-nothing, and the players have a record of nothing-and-190." It's safe to say that the caustic Cosell didn't regard Stengel with the same level of fondness that he would reserve for Muhammad Ali in later years.

Bring in What's-His-Name

Casey Stengel could be downright stubborn, to the point that some wondered whether his stubbornness was sometimes a way to hide his ignorance. An example of Stengel's odd behavior can be found on August 11, 1963, when he visited the mound to change pitchers. Having decided to remove Jay Hook from the game, Stengel refused to tell home plate umpire Stan Landes the name of the reliever he had chosen to take the ball.

"Wait till he comes on the mound," Stengel instructed Landes, "and then I'll tell you."

Not appreciating the suspense, Landes ejected Stengel from the game. After being given the heave-ho, Stengel elected not to wait on the mound for the reliever whose identity he may or may not have known. By the time the reliever reached the mound, Stengel was long gone. And the name of the reliever? It was obscure left-hander Grover Powell, who was making one of only 20 major league appearances in his career. Perhaps Stengel didn't know his name after all.

A Banner Idea

Due to the franchise's early on-field ineptitude, members of the Mets' front office had to use more ingenuity than the cross-town Yankees when it came to conjuring publicity and arranging promotions. The level of creativity never reached greater heights than on September 15, 1963, when the Mets debuted "Banner Day." The event allowed fans a chance to create and display their homemade banners during an on-field parade. It became the trademark and highlight of the team's promotional calendar.

The front office also deserved credit for allowing some banners that featured what might be called humorously negative content. During the first Banner Day, a few fans displayed a large sign that offered up a question, and an immediate answer: "Know Why The Mets Are Such Good Losers? Practice Makes Perfect." Other fans incorporated rhyme into their banners, such as the one that paid tribute to first baseman Tim Harkness with the following piece of poetry: "Hit One Into The Darkness, Harkness." And then there were some obvious fans of the Peanuts cartoon, and specifically, the frustrated character of Charlie Brown. Their advice was simple. "Good Grief, Let's Go Mets."

The Krane

No player is more associated with the Mets of the 1960s than first baseman Ed Kranepool. As a 17-year-old out of James Monroe High School in the Bronx, he signed with the expansion franchise in 1962, receiving a tidy bonus of $85,000 in the process. Given his strong left-handed swing and his New York roots, Kranepool almost immediately became a favorite of both the organization and its newly adopted fans. Just a few weeks after signing his first professional contract, he joined the team during its first year of existence and remained with the club off and on through the championship season of 1969, making him the last of the original Mets. Known as a blue-collar player, Kranepool never worked harder than he did during an unusual stretch in 1964, when he became an ironman of sorts at both the minor league and major league levels.

Having started the season at Triple-A Buffalo, Kranepool played both games—and every inning—of a doubleheader on May 30. The Mets then recalled Kranepool the next day, with Casey Stengel immediately inserting him into the lineup as the starting first baseman. Even though Kranepool played all nine innings of the first game of another doubleheader, Stengel didn't rest him in Game 2 against the Giants; he penciled his name into the lineup card, once again installing him at first base. Kranepool remained in action for another 23 consecutive innings (or the equivalent of two regular games plus another five innings), as the Mets and Giants played a marathon of a nightcap. (At the time, the doubleheader set a record, taking just over nine hours and 50 minutes to complete.)

By the time the doubleheader against San Francisco had ended, Kranepool had played a grand total of 50 innings over the span of 34 hours, or the equivalent of nearly six regulation games in the course of two days. (No official records are kept on such matters, especially when they involve a crossover between minor and major league games, but the 50 innings must have set some sort of professional baseball record.) And while Kranepool sometimes complained about being platooned by Mets managers over the years, he certainly had no reason to cite a lack of playing time on May 30 and May 31 of 1964.

Shea Hey!

Shea Stadium has served as the Mets' home ballpark since 1964, but hasn't always been known by its current name. Originally called Flushing Meadows Stadium (referring to its specific location in the borough of Queens), the park was renamed just one year before its first season of official use by the Mets. In a bill signed by New York City Mayor Robert Wagner, the ballpark officially became known as William A. Shea Municipal Stadium on February 4, 1963. The decision made the ballpark name a tribute to Bill Shea, a New York-based lawyer who had played an instrumental role in bringing National League baseball back to the city after the departures of the Dodgers and Giants.

On April 16, 1964, Shea officially christened the new ballpark by pouring water from both the Harlem River and the Gowanus Canal onto the infield. The next day, the Mets opened the park by losing a 4-3 decision to the Pittsburgh Pirates. The loss justified recent comments by Casey Stengel, who had said that "the park is lovelier than my team."

Due to the length of the stadium's name, the words "William A." and "Municipal" were eventually dropped in common everyday usage, giving birth to the more popular references of "Shea Stadium" or merely "Shea." Unfortunately, the ballpark's namesake is mostly forgotten today by fans who should be aware of Bill Shea's work in making the Mets a major league reality.

Murphy's Law

Not much went right on the field for the Mets in their earliest seasons. They didn't have much talent to begin with, and the talent they managed to acquire through trades or their fledgling farm system often faded. Steve Treder, a writer for *The Hardball Times* and one of the best baseball historians on the internet, recalls three promising Mets who flopped rather unexpectedly:

Big George Altman: "Acquired from the St. Louis Cardinals in exchange for Roger Craig," says Treder, "the slugging Altman came to the Mets after hitting .303, .318, and .274 the previous three seasons. He was counted on to be the big bat in the middle of the Mets order in 1964, but flopped terribly, to just a .230 batting average with nine homers."

Charlie Neal: "He was one of the better infielders in the National League from 1957 to '59," Treder recalls, "especially in 1959 when he was a bona fide star and led the Los Angeles Dodgers to the pennant, Neal slumped badly in 1960 and 1961. The Mets purchased him, and he had a decent year for their dreadful '62 team, hitting .260 with 11 homers. Then he flopped again in '63; the Mets sent him to the Cincinnati Reds, and his major league career was quickly over."

Johnny Lewis: "His raw numbers of the low-offense era of the mid-1960s may not look like much, but the 25-year-old Johnny Lewis had a pretty good year in the Mets' outfield in 1965," Treder says. "He hit .245 with 15 homers and 59 walks.

He then flopped hard to a .193 average in 1966, and was gone from the majors in early 1967."

The Gondola

Lindsey Nelson was best known for his outrageously loud sports coats, but his colorful behavior also extended into the area of unusual broadcast locations. When the Mets ventured into Houston to play their first series at the Astrodome in April of 1965, Nelson came up with an offbeat and somewhat courageous idea: he would broadcast part of the game from a small gondola hanging from the highest point of the Astrodome, a lofty 208 feet from the ground. Equipped with a walkie-talkie and a head set that allowed him to communicate with fellow Mets broadcasters Ralph Kiner and Bob Murphy, Nelson performed play-by-play and color duties in the seventh and eighth inning of a 12-9 loss to the newly named Astros.

Prior to the game, Astrodome ground rules established that the gondola would be "in play" throughout the game, meaning that any ball that struck the gondola would be considered a live ball. Fortunately, no batted balls hit the gondola, sparing Nelson the perilous duty of having to elude a pop-up while trying to maintain his safe balance in the gondola. Even more thankfully, Nelson never attempted a similar stunt again, returning to the relative safety of the Astrodome press box in future games.

Let's Get It Right

For years, this story has been told with the following details: On May 23, 1965, the Mets' Ron Swoboda took his position in right field wearing a batting helmet on his foot. The reason? After an unsuccessful at-bat, Swoboda had attempted to kick his helmet, only to get his foot stuck. Unable to remove the helmet, Swoboda was ordered to take the field by manager Casey Stengel.

Well, that turned out to be WRONG. During an interview with me on MLB Radio, Swoboda informed me that I had made a few mistakes in re-living this tall tale. According to Swoboda, the story should have read something like this:

On May 23, 1965, the Mets' Ron Swoboda was involved in a comical incident in a game in St. Louis. After making a three-base error on a routine fly ball to right field, followed by an unsuccessful at-bat, Swoboda tried to stomp on his helmet, only to get his foot stuck. Upset by the rookie's show of temper, manager Casey Stengel removed Swoboda from the game and ordered him to the clubhouse.

And that's the RIGHT version. A check of the box score for that day supports Swoboda's claim. Swoboda was indeed removed from the game, replaced by the speedy Johnny Lewis, who moved over from center field. Journeyman Billy Cowan took Lewis's place in center, with Danny Napoleon inserted into the left-field slot by a rather perturbed Stengel. So what's the lesson here? If you're going to take a swing or a swipe at your helmet, make sure you don't get your hand or foot stuck in it.

Hiller's Lesson

Darren Viola is one of the key contributors to arguably the best baseball site on the internet: www.baseballprimer.com. A longtime follower of New York sports, Viola goes by "Repoz" over the internet, in dedication to former Yankee outfielder Roger Repoz, and has attended more games at Shea Stadium and Yankee Stadium than most mortals. As a fan who grew up with the Mets and the Yankees in the 1960s, Viola recalls an intriguing encounter with former Mets second baseman Chuck Hiller, who passed away in 2004 while serving in the team's front office.

"It had to be 1965 or '66 on a dank day at Shea Stadium," Viola says, "when I was scrounging autographs during batting practice ... *with a stadium-provided pencil!* [I forgot my pen that day.] The Mets were playing the Cubs and I had gotten autographs from Ernie Banks, Ron Santo, and Billy Williams. So switching over to the Mets' side, Hiller looked at my scorecard in pencil and said something along the lines: 'You really should have these in pen.' Needless to say, it poured late in the game and me and my pals took off for the train—using our boffo-looking Banks/Santo/Williams scorecard as a hat.

"Hat gone ... scorecard gone ... autographs gone ... lesson kept."

A Hip Check to Casey

For years, critics of Casey Stengel felt that he should have been relieved of his duties as Mets manager because of his advancing age or because of a belief that changes in the modern game had "passed by" his old school ways.

As it turned out, neither reason resulted in his departure as manager, at least not directly.

In the late-night hours of a July evening, Stengel suffered a broken hip, either while innocently getting out of a car or during a boisterous postgame celebration at Toots Shor's. (The exact details of the broken hip incident remain a mystery.) The injury to the soon-to-be 75-year-old Stengel forced him to undergo surgery for a hip joint replacement, knocking him out of the managerial chair for the rest of the year and setting the stage for a takeover by coach Wes Westrum. One month later, convinced that Stengel's health would no longer allow him to manage, the Mets' front office announced the retirement of the "Old Perfessor." Stengel handled the announcement philosophically while offering his own brand of blunt logic.

"If I can't run out there and take a pitcher out," Stengel told the assembled media, "I'm not capable of continuing as manager."

Unlike many other Stengel proclamations, this one made complete sense. It was time for Casey to step aside, paving the way for his almost immediate election to the Hall of Fame.

The Franchise Lottery

If the Atlanta Braves hadn't broken the rules, "The Franchise" might never have landed in New York. In February of 1966, the Braves announced the signing of amateur right-hander Tom Seaver, a star pitcher at the University of Southern California. Not so fast, ruled Commissioner William "Spike" Eckert. On March 2, Eckert declared that the Braves' contract with Seaver be deemed null and void since it broke a basic baseball rule: no college player could sign with a major league team while his collegiate season remained in progress. Eckert then offered an invitation to any other team interested in Seaver: match the Braves' original offer of $40,000 and earn the right to participate in a lottery that would give the winner the first chance to negotiate with Seaver. The Mets, Cleveland Indians, and Philadelphia Phillies all accepted Eckert's offer, with the names of each of the three teams thrown into a hat. On April 3, Eckert presided over the lottery and presto—Seaver chose the Mets' name from the hat.

The Mets immediately started negotiations with Seaver, offered him $10,000 more than the Braves originally had, and signed him to a $50,000 bonus. "Tom Terrific" could just as easily have wound up with the Indians or the Phillies (imagine an eventual tandem of Seaver and Steve Carlton in Philadelphia), but luck—and the direction of Spike Eckert's hand—resided with the Mets on that fateful day.

Tom Terrific to the Rescue

For Mets play-by-play broadcaster Howie Rose, who also covered the team through his popular *Mets Extra* program on WFAN Radio, there's little doubt as to which player he admired most during his childhood years as a baseball fan.

"Unquestionably, it was Tom Seaver," says Rose, both a lifelong fan of the Mets and one of the most respected historians of Mets culture. "Seaver came to the Mets in 1967, when they were in their sixth season in the National League, and had been just a miserable doormat before his arrival. There was this inescapable culture of losing, and at least among their fans, a growing restlessness that this acceptance of losing was going to be something permanent."

Prior to Seaver, no player had given Mets fans hope of achieving the level of superstardom associated with a Hall of Fame icon.

"Although they had good young players that were starting to develop at the major league level—like Cleon Jones, Bud Harrelson, and Ed Kranepool—Seaver almost from the beginning was special," says Rose. "I think that people who watched him as a rookie got the sense that they had finally developed a player who was capable of doing special things, and therefore capable of helping the Mets achieve some pretty good things on their own along the way.

**Tom Seaver—the signature player in the history of the Mets'
franchise.** PHOTO FILE/Landov

"No one obviously expected what was to happen two years
later (in the form of a world championship), but clearly watching
the development of Tom Seaver, watching a Hall of Famer grow
as a New York Met was quite a thrill, even for a kid."

Koosman for Patek

Without Jerry Koosman, the Mets would have been hard pressed to win their first world championship in 1969. They almost faced that predicament—only to be saved by another team's rejection of a trade offer involving "Kooz."

Unsatisfied with their shortstop play in 1968, the Mets allegedly offered Koosman to the Pittsburgh Pirates for a highly regarded middle infield prospect named Freddie Patek. In retrospect, the deal seemed like a no-brainer for the Pirates, who certainly would have benefited from having an excellent left-handed starter near the top of their rotation for the next decade or so. At the time, however, the Pirates harbored concerns over the health of their veteran shortstop, Gene Alley, who suffered from chronic shoulder problems. With Alley's long-term availability a concern, the Pirates rejected the Mets' offer of a one-for-one deal.

In looking back at the proposed deal, fans of the Mets can thank the Pirates for their hesitancy in making a trade. Without Koosman, the Mets would have lacked a left-handed starter in their otherwise all-right-handed rotation. More importantly, they would have had to make do without an ideal No. 2 starter—a perfect complement to staff ace Tom Seaver. And then there was the shortstop situation. With young Buddy Harrelson about to emerge as one of the best fielding middle infielders in the National League, the Mets really didn't need Patek after all. And they certainly didn't need him at the cost of one of the league's most effective left-handed starting pitchers.

Bob Johnson

Not all of the Mets' top young pitching prospects of the late 1960s found long-term success in the major leagues. Originally drafted by the New York Mets in 1964, Bob Johnson was a hard-throwing right-hander who had overcome adversity in making himself one of the game's top pitching prospects. In 1967, Johnson had barely averted tragedy while pitching for the Mets' farm team in Williamsport of the Eastern League. Johnson suffered a severely fractured leg in a serious motorcycle accident.

"I was going along pretty good when the bike skidded on about three feet of gravel on the road," Johnson told *The Sporting News.* "My left leg was mangled."

The mishap left his leg so badly damaged that two doctors recommended amputation of at least part of the limb. Fortunately, another doctor decided that the broken leg could be saved. The decision ultimately saved Johnson's career. As the young pitcher recovered from the injury, he promised himself that he would never drive another motorcycle during his professional career.

Two years later, Johnson made his major league debut as part of the "Miracle Mets," but his career as a Met would not endure for long. After the 1969 season, the Mets included him as a throw-in in the disastrous Amos Otis-for-Joe Foy deal. Johnson, through no fault of his own, had become involved in one of the most one-sided trades in franchise history.

Although now mostly forgotten after his retirement, Johnson would pitch well in his one season with the Kansas City Royals, who then used him as off-season trade bait. Dealt to the Pittsburgh Pirates for shortstop Freddie Patek, Johnson became a secondary member of the world champion Bucs in 1971, serving as both a starter and long reliever.

Johnson followed up the Pirates' championship season by posting one of his best major league campaigns in 1972, forging an earned run average of 2.96 as a long reliever and spot starter. But then in 1973 he found himself mired in mediocrity. After the season, the Bucs traded him to the Cleveland Indians. Once one of baseball's most pursued young pitchers, Johnson had seen his on-field value depreciate to a career low.

Later in his career, Johnson announced publicly that he had struggled with a severe drinking problem. Johnson said he had begun drinking with the Royals in 1970, and only increased his drinking habit during his three-year stay with the Pirates.

"It was affecting my behavior. I was saying things I shouldn't have been saying. I was hung over in the clubhouse most of the time," Johnson revealed in a 1977 interview with New York *Daily News* baseball writer Phil Pepe.

In May of 1974, Johnson's heavy drinking led to an episode of erratic behavior aboard the Indians' team flight from Detroit to Dallas. Johnson became angered when the flight's departure was delayed and proceeded to argue with stewardesses about a mix-up in seating assignments.

"I was snockered," Johnson admitted to Pepe.

Johnson abruptly walked off the plane during a stopover in Indianapolis. The Indians fined Johnson a reported $500 and waived him later that season.

In October 1975, Johnson vowed never to take another drink. Two years later, he made it back to the major leagues for a brief but unsuccessful stint with the Atlanta Braves. "I knew that it was time for me to call it quits," Johnson told *Sports Collectors Digest* in 1997. "I didn't just want to hang on."

For Johnson, a career that had begun with so much promise ended with a lifetime record of just 28-34. Unlike Tom Seaver and Nolan Ryan, there would be no place in Cooperstown for

Johnson's once-golden right arm. Unlike Jerry Koosman and Tug McGraw, Johnson would become one of the forgotten hurlers on the famed young pitching staff that carried New York to victory in 1969—and mostly unknown to future generations of Mets fans.

Early Signs of Trouble

Mets fans know all too well about the tragic loss of arguably their best manager ever, Gil Hodges, who died from a massive heart attack during the spring of 1972. Yet, Hodges's heart troubles actually began four years earlier when he suffered what was diagnosed as a "mild" heart attack.

Stricken late in 1968, Hodges was forced to the sidelines for the final week of the regular season. The Mets named pitching coach Rube Walker as interim manager for the balance of the season, but announced that they expected Hodges to return in time for the start of the 1969 campaign. Given a clean bill of health, Hodges reassumed command of the Mets in the spring of 1969 and proceeded to put together one of the greatest single-season managerial jobs of all time—guiding the "Miracle Mets" to the most unlikeliest of world championships.

The Great Gil Hodges

During his 20-year major league career, Tom Seaver played for a number of managers that he liked and respected, including Tony La Russa and John McNamara, but none registered quite as highly as Gil Hodges.

"You grow very close to certain managers that you play for. Gil was the most important guy in my life at the professional level," says Seaver, who was in his second season with the Mets in 1968. "And I love to tell the story about one day when Gil called me into the office. Gil had this reputation of being a hero in the south Pacific in World War II. He was a Marine. We were both Marines. He didn't take any guff. He was a man's man. And there was only one way to play, and that was his way as a professional all the time. In 1968, I pitched a game against the Giants. I was ahead, 7-0, and then I turned around and the score was 7-6. I had gotten a little big for my britches and all of a sudden it was 7-6. I ended up winning the game—luckily. I went into the locker and was getting undressed when [pitching coach] Rube Walker came over and said, 'Gil wants to see you.' That ain't good right there. I stuck my head in his office door and said, 'You want to see me.' He said, 'Yeah, come on in.' That's even worse. Then he said, 'Close the door.' And that's *real bad.*

"I went in and sat down. He said to me, 'Your approach to the game today was miserable. You showed no respect. You should be ashamed of yourself.' He literally chewed me out for about 10 minutes. He told me very simplistically, 'I don't care if it's April or September, if its Los Angeles on Tuesday or Chicago on Sunday, it doesn't make any difference in how you go about your business.' He impressed that on me about three different ways and then he said, 'You're done.'

"I got that lesson in the middle of my second year in the big leagues—and never forgot it. Never."

CHAPTER TWO

1969 and Beyond

Trading for Torre

When it comes to the Mets, Joe Torre is most associated with the franchise's futility of the mid-to-late 1970s. Yet, Torre almost became part of the club's first championship run in 1969. It almost happened—if only the Mets had been able to satisfy the Atlanta Braves on the trade front.

Coming off a frustrating 1968 season, the Mets' front office realized the team needed some offensive help. The Mets had struggled in one-run games, losing 37 of 63 such outcomes. With many of the games falling into the category of low scoring, it was hard to blame the pitching. Even in the "Year of the Pitcher," in which no major league team scored 700 runs, the Mets' offense—second to last in the National League with a scant 473 runs—stood in line as the real culprit. Without any top-notch offensive prospects ready to contribute, the Mets realized they would have to seek help outside of the organization. They talked to the Philadelphia Phillies about the talented but troubled Richie

Allen, but couldn't satisfy the Phillies with enough talent in return. The Montreal Expos offered power-hitting first baseman Donn Clendenon in exchange for pitchers Gary Gentry and Jim McAndrew, but the Mets considered the price too steep.

Next up came the Atlanta Braves, who were willing to listen to offers for hard-hitting catcher-third baseman Joe Torre. The Mets certainly had interest in Torre, a native New Yorker who had also expressed an interest in playing for the Mets. All that was left was to convince Braves general manager Paul Richards to make a deal. Willing to give up Torre for the right price, Richards reportedly asked for a package that would include catcher Jerry Grote and first baseman Ed Kranepool.

The Mets considered the trade, which would have given them a bonafide offensive star. On the down side, they would have been forced to give up two starting position players for one, thereby leaving a hole in their starting lineup. Ultimately, the Mets considered the asking price for Torre too high and left Richards's offer on the table. No deal. A few weeks later, during the spring of 1969, Richards would trade Torre to the St. Louis Cardinals for future Hall of Famer Orlando Cepeda. Torre's arrival in New York would have to wait until the start of the 1975 season.

The Cold Corner

If the Mets had somehow been able to acquire Joe Torre without giving up both Jerry Grote and Ed Kranepool, they could have placed him at third base and solved a longstanding problem for the organization. By the end of the 1968 season, the Mets had used a total of 39 third basemen—or an average of nearly six different third basemen per season. Only a few of the third basemen had even approached mediocrity for the Mets, while most of them found themselves mired in misery.

Prior to the 1969 season, Mets beat writer Jack Lang of the *Long Island Press* and *The Sporting News* contributed a memorable one-line description about one of the many Mets failures at the hot corner. "Danny [Napoleon] was no better at third than the real Napoleon was at Waterloo." Originally an outfielder, Napoleon played seven games at third base for the Mets in 1965 before convincing the Mets to end the experiment. Over the span of two seasons and 130 at-bats, Napoleon batted .162 with no home runs and an on-base percentage of .227.

Torre might not have provided the Mets with anything more than average defensive play at third base, but his hitting skills would have made Mets fans forget about Napoleon and his company of 38 third-base pretenders. With Torre out of New York's focus and instead a member of the Cardinals, the Mets would turn to young Wayne "Red" Garrett as their semi-regular third baseman in 1969—and the 40th third baseman in the franchise's history. Though hardly a star, the left-handed hitting Garrett would give the Mets a decent platoon third baseman for several years, including a career-best 16 home runs during the pennant-winning season of 1973.

Big Train

On January 22, 1969, a trade between the Houston Astros and the expansion Montreal Expos indirectly helped the Mets win the National League East. In making their first trade as a franchise, the Expos dealt first baseman Donn "Big Train" Clendenon and three other players to the Astros for star outfielder Rusty Staub. The Mets probably didn't give much thought to the deal at the time, other than recalling what they considered an exorbitant asking price of Gary Gentry and Jim McAndrew. More to the point, the trade of Clendenon didn't look like it would have much affect on the Mets. The Expos figured to be a bad team in their first year of existence while the Astros played in the other, newly created Western Division.

Well, the trade turned out to be the best thing for the Mets. When Clendenon refused to report to Houston, the Expos restructured the trade and brought back the slugging first base-man—albeit with something other than open arms. Unhappy in Montreal, Clendenon remained on the trade block. On June 15, the day of baseball's trading deadline, the Mets took advantage of the situation by dealing infielder Kevin Collins and three minor league pitchers to the Expos for Clendenon.

Of the players dealt, only young right-hander Steve Renko did anything of consequence for the expansion Expos, while the right-handed hitting Clendenon paid immediate dividends for the Mets. At first employed by Gil Hodges as a platoon partner for Ed Kranepool before becoming the everyday solution at first base, Clendenon strengthened the Mets' lineup against left-handed pitching and deepened a relatively thin and inexperienced bench. In 72 games with the Mets, Clendenon hit 12 home runs with 37 RBIs, helping the Mets over the final three and a half months of the regular season. Even more significantly, Clendenon became the centerpiece of the Mets' offense during the World Series. In Game 1 against the Baltimore Orioles, Clendenon doubled and singled—representing the Mets' lone hitting standout in a Series-opening loss. In Game 2, he powered a solo home run that lifted the Mets to a 2-1 victory. Clendenon then homered in Game 4, and again in the clinching Game 5, as the New Yorkers finalized their stunning upset of the seemingly invincible Birds of Baltimore.

Swoboda and the Straitjacket

In early February, the New York Baseball Writers staged their annual preseason show, which featured an array of performances, some of which might have been loosely regarded as "entertainment." As one of the most colorful members of the Mets, Ron Swoboda seemed like a natural to participate in the show. Swoboda waddled onto the stage wearing a straitjacket and offering a promise of being able to free himself within the span of a few moments. As part of the act, Swoboda ate some "Big Yaz" bread (in homage to Carl Yastrzemski's Triple Crown season of 1967), which would supposedly give him the strength to extricate himself from the confines of the jacket within a mere 10 seconds.

Not surprisingly, the 10 seconds came and went with Swoboda still shackled in the straitjacket. By the time the show's "grand finale" took place, Swoboda still couldn't free himself. Presumably, one of the writers untangled Swoboda before letting him drive home.

Meal Money for the Dog

Whereas Ron Swoboda had failed in his efforts to entertain the writers, right-handed pitcher Gary Gentry did his best to entertain the press corps with his own sideshow during the spring of 1969. Gentry brought an unexpected guest to the Mets' spring training site in St. Petersburg, Florida—a 150-pound St. Bernard. Gentry proudly declared to the media that his 13-month-old pet consumed about five pounds of meat per day, which prompted some writers to speculate about an increase in Gentry's meal money. Mets general manager Johnny Murphy quickly quieted such rumors.

"[Team owner] Mrs. [Joan] Payson doesn't have enough dough to feed that thing," Murphy explained, perhaps only half-kiddingly.

Pucci

The presence of Gary Gentry's St. Bernard brought back memories of the previous spring, when Tug McGraw brought his pet dog to spring training in St. Petersburg. Affectionately named "Pucci," McGraw's dog wasn't as large as Gentry's, but caused far more trouble in the spring of 1968.

One day, Pucci ransacked the flowerbed located outside of Johnny Murphy's office, an event that didn't please the Mets' general manager. On another occasion, Pucci decided to use the sidewalk outside of coach Joe Pignatano's apartment as her own personal bathroom. Pignatano subsequently slipped on "the mess." If only Pucci had waited until the start of the regular season, she might have been able to christen Pignatano's bullpen vegetable garden at Shea Stadium.

Honest Hodges

During his tenure as manager of the Mets, Gil Hodges produced an array of reactions from his players. Loved by some, feared by many, and respected by all, Hodges thrived by motivating his Mets' teams to play hard while also emphasizing those fundamentals he considered crucial to on-field success.

Hodges could also be blunt when asked to describe his team's performance. In an era before political correctness, and at a time when managers still had enough authority to offer public criticisms of their players, Hodges believed that his team occa-

Few Mets have been as colorful, outspoken, and honest as Ron "Rocky" Swoboda. Focus on Sport/Getty Images

sionally needed to hear a brutally honest assessment of its short-comings. Such harsh public airings occurred even during the championship season of 1969. Playing in an early-season series against the Astros, the Mets lost all three games at Houston's Astrodome. In the process, Mets batters struck out 31 times, a total Hodges deemed unacceptable.

"They all looked like wooden soldiers," Hodges told Jack Lang, the Mets' correspondent for *The Sporting News* and a beat writer for the *Long Island Press,* in expressing anger over his team's inability to make contact.

The Removal

On July 30, Gil Hodges reached one of the most fervent boiling points of his managerial career. The day started out poorly when the Mets lost the first game of a doubleheader, an embarrassing 16-3 loss to the Astros, which included two Houston grand slams in the ninth inning. The Astros continued the onslaught in the second game; pounding out 10 runs in the third inning. With the Mets' poor performance already having put Hodges in a foul mood, the manager made his way toward the mound to make an apparent pitching change in the midst of the latest Houston outburst.

Hodges reached the mound, but didn't stop walking. Instead, he continued to tread slowly toward the left side of the infield, and then toward the outfield. Within a few moments, he met up with Cleon Jones, who had been slow in retrieving a ball that had been hit into the left-field corner. Hodges and Jones exchanged words, before the manager turned around and started to make his way back toward the dugout. Jones followed, his head turned downward, about 10 steps behind his displeased manager.

One of the true icons of the Mets—the great Gil Hodges.
Focus on Sport/Getty Images

In discussing the decision to remove Jones in the midst of the inning, Hodges explained that the left fielder's "leg was bothering him." No one believed Hodges. In truth, Hodges felt that Jones had not hustled in fielding the ball hit down the left-field line. Furious over what he considered lackadaisical play, Hodges felt that immediate removal from the game was suitable punishment.

The act of discipline failed to motivate the Mets—at least in the short term. They went on to lose the second game of the doubleheader, 11-5, and then suffered a shutout loss to Houston's Tom Griffin the next day. Yet, Hodges had succeeded in delivering an important message, overtly and demonstratively. *There was only one way to play the game, and that was to play hard all the time.* Judging by the team's eventual performance in August and September, the Mets' players seemed to grasp the relevance of Hodges's lesson.

A Daffy Double Play

Rod Gaspar was a role player on the 1969 Mets, a backup outfielder and a switch-hitting pinch-hitter. Like Dick McAuliffe of the Detroit Tigers, Gaspar batted out of an unusually wide stance at the plate, with his body facing almost directly toward the pitcher's mound. Yet, it was an unusual play that Gaspar made on defense from his position in the outfield that helped the Mets win an important game late in the 1969 season.

"We were playing San Francisco," Gaspar says in recalling the August 30 game at Candlestick Park. "I was playing left field late in the game. The score was tied in the bottom of the ninth inning. Willie McCovey was up and Tug [McGraw] was pitching. I figured they're not going to pitch to McCovey. McCovey was the league MVP that year, and I think they intentionally walked him more than any other player. There was this guy named Bob Burda, he was on first base, and I think there was one out. They decided to pitch to McCovey, and we did this thing called the McCovey shift. It was like the Ted Williams shift when everybody plays to right field. [Donn] Clendenon was on the line at first base. [Tommie] Agee is in center-right, and I'm over in left-center field, quite aways from the right-field line. Tug throws McCovey one of his screwballs and he hits it down to the left-field line. The bottom of the ninth inning, winning run on first base. As soon as he hits it, the guy [Burda] takes off. We were playing at Candlestick Park, which at the time had a grass field, and if you're familiar with the weather in San Francisco, you'd know that the field was wet. He hits a nine-iron down the left-field line, and it lands fair. As soon as he hit it, I took off. I knew that our only chance was to get to the ball. I knew the guy was going to try and score. The ball lands, and it sticks in the ground! I pick it up, and Burda's going around third; I pivoted, and threw a strike to [Clendenon, who threw the ball to Jerry] Grote at home. I didn't have an arm like [Roberto] Clemente, [Dave] Winfield, or Ollie Brown, but I think I led the league in double plays for outfielders that year. We got Burda pretty easy at home. I think it might have shocked Grote that I threw a strike and he forgot how many outs there were. He thought there were three outs, but it was only the second. He rolls the ball to the pitcher's mound. Meanwhile McCovey's rounding third, but Clendenon is behind it. Clendenon is a headstrong player. He throws it to third base, and nabs McCovey on third on a double play. We went on to win the game, 3-2. Bottom of the ninth, we got Burda at home plate and McCovey at third. It was a 7-3-2-3-5 double play."

From Darling Doormats
to Kings of Queens

On August 15, the Mets resided in third place in the National League's Eastern Division. Third place was a respectable standing for the perennially porous Mets, but first place, still nine and a half games away, seemed like it would have to wait until 1970 as part of Gil Hodges's rebuilding program.

With Hall of Fame talents like Ernie Banks, Billy Williams and Ferguson Jenkins, a lineup of veteran stars and a deep starting rotation, the Chicago Cubs seemed uncatchable at the top of the division. In addition to having the advantage in experience and talent, pure mathematics favored the Cubs, what with only seven weeks remaining in the regular season.

Those seven weeks provided the Mets with more than enough time to turn the fortunes of the baseball world over and upside down, much to the chagrin of the Cubs. As one former Met points out, the contrast between the Cubs' age and the Mets' youth played a part in determining the division.

"Leo Durocher was doing well with his veteran ballplayers," says Rod Gaspar, who appeared in 118 games as a reserve on the 1969 Mets. "According to stories [I heard], Leo was enjoying himself at that time, but the Cubs' pitching fell apart, and a young upstart team, the Mets, took their place. Our average age was only 25-26 years old. The majority of Durocher's starting lineup was All-Stars. Leo wore 'em out [by playing them every day].

"The Houston Astros gave us more problems than anybody. They kicked our butts all season. They beat us [sweeping a three-game series], but from then on, we went on to win 38 out of 49 ballgames."

That incredible run gave the Mets an eight-game lead in the Eastern Division by season's end. In other words, within a span of less than two months, the Mets had managed a turnaround of 17 and a half games in the standings.

Greetings from New York's Other Team

When the Mets took over first place in the National League East, all of New York took notice. Even the hated Yankees took pleasure in the Mets' unlikely climb from second-division stooges to postseason participants. Yankees president Michael Burke, offering enthusiastic support with a tinge of gallows humor, sent the following telegram to Mets chairman M. Donald Grant:

"Congratulations on being number one. Am rooting for you to hang in there and take all the marbles. As a New Yorker I am ecstatic, as a baseball person I am extremely pleased, and as a Yankee I consider suicide the easy option."

Taylor and Tug

Unlike most current-day championship teams, the 1969 Mets did not assign the role of closer or relief ace to just one man. Instead, Gil Hodges delegated late-inning authority to two stand-out relievers, right-hander Ron Taylor and left-hander Tug McGraw. Their pattern of usage was reflected in their statistics.

"We had almost identical records that year," Taylor recalls. "I was 9-4; Tug was 9-4 [actually 9-3]. We each had around 14 saves [Taylor had 13 and McGraw had 12]. We both had ERAs in the 2.00 range."

Taylor maintained his effectiveness with a workmanlike combination of sinkers and sliders, while McGraw often baffled opposing hitters with one of the game's best screwballs.

As co-firemen leading the Mets' relief corps, Taylor and McGraw developed a good relationship. "We spent a lot of time in the bullpen together," says Taylor. "We went to Vietnam together [on a goodwill tour] after the '69 Series." Yet, the personalities of Taylor and McGraw could not have been much different.

"I wish I could have been more like Tug McGraw," says the introverted Taylor. "I'm kind of a quiet and laid-back person. Tug was always up front and entertaining people."

An Encounter on the Mound

Like many of the 1969 Mets, Ron Taylor considers Gil Hodges the best manager he ever played for during his professional career. As a manager, Hodges believed in the importance of defining clear-cut roles for every player on the 25-man roster, something that members of the 1969 Mets appreciated.

"In spring training of 1969, everybody knew what their role was," Taylor says. "Everybody was quite happy with their role. Even more so when we started to win."

Hodges also possessed the courage to trust his players when their suggestions contradicted both his strategy and the bounds of logic. An incident during the 1969 season against the Atlanta Braves illustrates the point.

"Orlando Cepeda's in the on-deck circle, and Henry's [Hank Aaron] up," says Taylor, who had always struggled in head-to-head match ups against Cepeda. "So Hodges comes up to me and says, 'I want you to put Henry on and face Cepeda.'

"I said, 'No. I want Aaron.'

"Hodges said, 'You *what?*' I knew he was angry. When he got angry, that jugular vein popped out of his neck. He said, 'You want to pitch to Aaron?'

"I said, 'Yeah.'

"So Hodges said, 'You better get him out.'"

Taylor did, retiring Aaron on an infield grounder.

"So I come back to the dugout and sit down. I'm looking down at Hodges," Taylor says. "He comes up to me and says, 'You know, you're crazier than I thought.'"

A Close Call

"Missed it by *that* much."

That was perhaps the most memorable catch phrase uttered by Maxwell Smart (as played by Don Adams) on the brilliant 1960s TV comedy, *Get Smart*.

Tommie Agee might have been saying similar words during Game 2 of the 1969 National League Championship Series. With the Mets holding a precarious 9-6 lead over the Atlanta Braves, Agee led off third base as Cleon Jones stepped into the batter's box against side-arming Cecil Upshaw. Opting to surprise the Braves with an attempted steal of home, Agee bolted for the plate. Jones, wanting to distract catcher Bob Didier, decided to swing at the pitch with the intent of missing the ball. Somehow (and this is almost beyond explanation) Jones made contact with the pitch, hitting a searing line drive down the third base line. The ball sailed past Agee, narrowly missing his head by about 20 inches. By *that* much.

In another stroke of fortune, the ball landed foul. And why was that fortunate? Later in the at-bat, Jones once again made solid contact, this time pounding a two-run homer to give the Mets their final margin of victory in an 11-6 win.

A Good Talker

Ron "Rocky" Swoboda is best remembered for the headlong, fully extended, backhanded catch that he made against Brooks Robinson in Game 4 of the 1969 World Series. It's a play that ranks among the five best catches in postseason history, a play that some baseball observers regard even more highly than Willie Mays's legendary over-the-shoulder catch in the 1954 World Series. Yet, the outgoing Swoboda also made his mark in Mets history through his abilities to communicate humorously with the New York press, often a difficult task in a media market the size of New York. As Swoboda said on the occasion of his 25th birthday in 1969: "I'm the only 25-year-old has-been in baseball."

For one Mets broadcaster, any opportunity to interview Swoboda could simply not be missed.

"My favorite interview, the guy who I enjoyed talking to more than any other, and they all came at Old-Timers events or other events that took place long after he stopped playing, was Ron Swoboda," says Howie Rose, who has interviewed hundreds of Mets players in his various broadcast roles with WFAN Radio. "I've never done an interview with Swoboda that didn't end with me wishing that we had more time to talk, even if we had talked for 10 or 15 minutes. I find him to be a fascinating guy, brutally honest, tremendously introspective, and very, very insightful."

After his playing days, Swoboda became a sports anchor for a New York City television station, but has never landed a position as a broadcaster with a major league team.

"I'm surprised that he hasn't hooked on with a big league club as a full-time broadcaster," says Rose. "I think with the right training as a baseball announcer, he could have been a real good one. I've never enjoyed an interview subject more than I did Ron Swoboda."

The Shoe Polish Affair

Considered a monumental mismatch by most objective observers, the 1969 World Series produced one of the most decided upsets in major league history, as the Mets surprised the mighty Baltimore Orioles in five games.

The decisive game of the Series also provided an unusual moment. With the Mets trailing, 3-0, in the sixth, Orioles' left-hander Dave McNally unfurled a hard-breaking curve that swept down and in on Cleon Jones. The Mets' left fielder maintained that he had been hit, but home plate umpire Lou DiMuro called the pitch a ball. A few moments later, Mets manager Gil Hodges emerged from the dugout holding a ball with a mark of shoe polish on it. According to Hodges, the shoe polish offered conclusive proof that the pitch had hit Jones in the foot. Although DiMuro had no way of knowing when or how the shoe polish had made its way on to the ball—or whether it was even *the ball* in question—he awarded Jones first base. (The play—and DiMuro's decision—reminded some observers of a similar incident involving Nippy Jones in the 1957 World Series.) Donn Clendenon followed with a two-run homer, beginning an unlikely New York comeback. The Mets scored three more runs in the seventh and eighth to win the first championship in the franchise's brief eight-year history.

Agee for Yaz

In 1969, Tommie Agee hit 26 home runs and won a Gold Glove for his defensive prowess in center field. And then in the World Series, he made two remarkable catches to help preserve a Game 3 victory against the Baltimore Orioles and retain momentum in a Series the Mets would eventually win. Yet, the Mets' championship run almost didn't happen. The Mets might not have won either the National League pennant or the world championship if a proposed trade had been made, one that would have prevented Agee from becoming a Met in the first place. Acquired in a multi-player deal with the Chicago White Sox, Agee was originally supposed to have been traded to the Boston Red Sox in a blockbuster deal—for Hall of Fame outfielder Carl Yastrzemski. The White Sox and Red Sox came close to completing the one-for-one swap, but Red Sox owner Tom Yawkey balked at the last minute, unwilling to give up Yaz, one of his favorite players. Yawkey's veto prevented the Red Sox from making what would have been one of the worst trades in franchise history—and indirectly helped the Mets in eventually acquiring the steadiest lynchpin to their 1969 championship team.

Foy the Flop

The 1969 season is regarded by many Mets fans as the greatest in the history of New York's youngest major league franchise. Unfortunately, the aftermath of the Mets' first world championship did not produce the wisest of off-season trade strategies.

On December 3, 1969, the Mets' front office engineered one of the worst trades in the history of the National League expansion franchise. With a glut of starting outfielders and an absence of a quality major league third baseman, the Mets sent youthful fly chaser Amos Otis to the Kansas City Royals. In exchange, they acquired 26-year-old third baseman Joe Foy, a talented player who had flashed an appealing combination of speed and power in his young career. Otis had batted only .151 in 48 games for the "Miracle Mets" and had failed miserably in an attempt to convert to third base, an experiment that the Mets would come to regret. Reestablished by the Royals as a center

Arguably the greatest defensive center fielder in Mets history, Tommie Agee provided nearly flawless fielding in 1969.
Focus on Sport/Getty Images

fielder, Otis would spend 14 seasons with Kansas City and finish his career with 193 home runs and 341 stolen bases.

In the meantime, Foy would last only one lackluster season with the Mets, his once-promising career seemingly plagued by rumored problems with alcohol and illegal drugs. After an unproductive season in New York, the Mets dumped Foy on the lowly Washington Senators, where his major career would end abruptly in the midst of the 1971 season—at the age of 28.

A Front Office Tragedy

Sadly, the health of general manager Johnny Murphy did not permit him much time to savor the first world championship in the history of the franchise. On January 14, as he continued to make preparations for the 1970 season, Murphy suffered a fatal heart attack at the age of 61. Though often overshadowed by the antics of one manager (Casey Stengel) and the success of another (Gil Hodges), Murphy played a large role in laying out the blueprint for the Mets' climb to postseason glory. He engineered trades for slugging first baseman Donn Clendenon, quiet middle infielder Al Weis, and dynamic outfielder Tommie Agee—three integral members of the 1969 team. Murphy also resisted the temptation to trade any of the Mets' best homegrown young pitchers (such as Tom Seaver, Jerry Koosman, and Nolan Ryan) for the immediate gratification of established veteran talent.

The death of Murphy forced the Mets to scramble to find an immediate replacement. Electing to stay in-house, the Mets tabbed farm director Bob Scheffing as Murphy's successor. Scheffing, well regarded as the overseer of the Mets' highly productive minor league system, would not achieve a similar level of success as the team's No. 1 baseball executive.

Funny Man Ray

The last trade engineered by Johnny Murphy netted the Mets veteran left-hander Ray Sadecki, who became a valuable part of the pitching staff while switching between starting and relief roles. Sadecki also brought some humor to the Mets, teaming with another veteran left-hander to form a comedic clubhouse duo.

"Ray Sadecki and Jerry Koosman were like a broken record," says former Mets ace Tom Seaver. "They'd say the same jokes *every* day. In the clubhouses, on the buses, at the hotels, *every* day. And they would laugh … and they would laugh."

Seaver remembers one joke in particular. "Ray said, 'Hey Koozie, it's pretty hot today.' 'That's right, Ray. It's pretty hot today. How hot is it, Ray?' 'Well, I saw a dog chasing a cat, and they were both walking.'"

As if the quality of the joke wasn't lacking to begin with, Sadecki and Koosman would repeat the joke at the team hotel. And then they would repeat it again on the team flight.

"After a while, it's like you got punch-drunk listening to this stuff," says Seaver.

Although their jokes evolved into a predictable refrain, Seaver enjoyed the comic efforts of both Sadecki and Koosman, and liked both as teammates. The addition of Sadecki in 1970 made the Mets clubhouse a more enjoyable place.

"Ray had a wonderful sense of humor," Seaver says. "He was a wonderful guy."

Seaver the Sage

Like most pitchers and pitching coaches who have been associated with Tom Seaver, Bill Monbouquette has great respect for the pitching knowledge and philosophies of the greatest pitcher in the history of the Mets franchise.

"I used to ask a lot of pitching coaches how they felt about the mechanics [used in throwing a baseball]," Monbouquette recalls. "Most of them would say, 'If it's not broke, don't fix it.' That wasn't the answer that I was looking for—because I believe in mechanics. So I asked Tom Seaver one day, 'Tommy, how do you feel about the mechanics of pitching?' And he said, simply put, 'Out of a sound delivery comes a sound arm.' You couldn't put it any more simply than that. And I said, 'I thank you very much. This is what I've been looking for.'

"Of course, he had the great delivery. Not only did he have nasty stuff, he had excellent command of all of his pitches. He was very aggressive. He wasn't afraid to throw the ball inside, or knock you off the plate. If one of your guys got drilled, he took care of business right away. And that's the way it's supposed to be. There wasn't any talk about it; it was just *done*."

Later in their careers, the paths of Monbouquette and Seaver crossed again. Monbouquette became the Mets' pitching coach and Seaver returned to the team after a five-and-a-half-year stint with the Cincinnati Reds. Monbouquette cherished the opportunity to work with the man known as "Tom Terrific."

"Seaver was so easy to coach. I asked him, 'You like to run, Tommy?' He said, 'No, but I have to.' I then asked him, 'Do you like the five-man rotation or a four-man rotation?' He said, 'I *hate* a four-man rotation. But I'll do it if I have to.' And so when we were running the pitchers and someone was goofing off, I didn't have to get on him; Tommy would get on him. He said, 'Hey, let's go. We have a job to do here.' He was such a great individual, easy to talk to."

A Throwback to Brooklyn

In choosing their original uniform colors of blue and orange in 1962, the Mets had paid homage to the memories of the former residents of New York, the Brooklyn Dodgers (who wore blue) and the New York Giants (who featured orange and brown). The Mets also established another interesting connection to the Brooklyn days when they made a trade with the Atlanta Braves after the 1970 season.

In a deal that the Mets hoped would strengthen their third-base situation, the team acquired infielder Bob Aspromonte from the Braves for pitcher Ron Herbel. Although Aspromonte was no more than a pedestrian player for most of his career, he was more notably known as one of the original members of the Houston Colt .45s. More significant to the Mets' line of thinking, Aspromonte represented the last active link to one of the city's earlier teams; he was the last remaining major leaguer to have played for the old Brooklyn Dodgers, who had relocated to Los Angeles in 1958.

As a freshly scrubbed 18-year-old, Aspromonte had broken into the major leagues by playing one game (and accumulating one at-bat) for Brooklyn in 1956, just one year after the "Bums" had claimed their first and only world championship while in Brooklyn. While the acquisition of Aspromonte struck a sentimental chord with baseball nostalgists in New York, the Mets hoped that Aspromonte would provide them with a tangible benefit, as well: a reliable platoon partner for left-handed hitting third-base novice Wayne Garrett.

Unfortunately, Aspromonte proved less useful than one of his predecessors at the hot corner, Ed Charles. Aspro batted a mere .225 with only five home runs in 104 games, prompting his retirement after the 1971 season. Yet, there was still something appropriate about Aspromonte ending his career with the Mets. As a native of Brooklyn, he had managed to both start and finish his major league career playing in the Big Apple. That gave him something in common with the far more legendary Willie Mays, who had started out as a member of the New York Giants before wrapping up his playing days as a New York Met.

Worst Trade Ever

After the 1971 season, the Mets felt they needed to address their long-persistent problem at third base. Wayne "Red" Garrett had yet to develop into the everyday solution, leaving the Mets looking for help on the trade market. Some members of the Mets front office felt that the team could deal from the strength of its deep pitching staff, with Nolan Ryan considered a logical candidate for the trade market. Knowing that the native Texan had never fully acclimated to pitching—or day-to-day life—in the Metropolitan area, the Mets felt that Ryan could become an attractive centerpiece to a package for a star third baseman.

At the 1971 winter meetings, the Mets found a suitable and willing trade partner—the California Angels. General manager Bob Scheffing sent Ryan and three minor league prospects to the Angels for shortstop Jim Fregosi, whom the Mets felt confident could make the transition to third base. A frequent All-Star, Fregosi had become the best player in the short 11-year history of the Angels franchise. Furthermore, he was still only 29 years of age at the time of the trade, leading the Mets to believe that he could fill the gaping abyss on the left side of the infield for the next several seasons.

So much for planning. Fregosi struggled badly in adjusting to third base, a position he had never played during his days in California. To make matters worse, he showed up to spring training out of shape and badly overweight. Fregosi also failed to lose weight during the season, instead enjoying the temptations of the New York City lifestyle. New York writers joked about the "middle tire" that appeared to circle its way around Fregosi's waist.

The Mets coaching staff took notice of Fregosi's lack of conditioning. The following spring, third base coach Eddie Yost offered a bluntly honest assessment of Fregosi's excess baggage.

"It wasn't just the extra weight he was carrying," Yost told Jack Lang of *The Sporting News* and the *Long Island Press*. "It was all that stuff around his middle. He couldn't move and he couldn't bend over."

With the ability to bend over one of the prerequisites of playing third base, Fregosi's performance in 1972 degraded to new levels of embarrassment.

To his credit, Fregosi committed himself to a healthier lifestyle that off season. He lost 15 pounds over the winter, reporting to spring training in 1973 at a far more manageable 192 pounds. Given his relatively young age (30) and a full year of transition to the National League under his tightened belt, the Mets believed that Fregosi would come much closer to matching his Halo days in California.

The loss of weight certainly helped, but Fregosi developed a sore arm during the spring, making it difficult for him to make the long throw from third base to first base. When shortstop Buddy Harrelson went down with an injury, Fregosi moved back to his original position, where he always seemed much more comfortable. He played well for awhile, especially in the field.

The success didn't last. Fregosi continued to struggle so much at the plate that Yogi Berra benched him, replacing him with the younger and more athletic Teddy Martinez. With frustrated fans joking that Jim Fregosi had somehow become Bela Lugosi (of *Dracula* fame), the Mets ended the agony by trading the former All-Star to the Texas Rangers. The Mets didn't even acquire a player in return for Fregosi, just a few thousand dollars in cash.

It Gets Worse

The Nolan Ryan-for-Jim Fregosi swap ranks as one of the most one-sided deals of all time. To make matters worse, the Mets actually gave the Angels *three* other players in the trade. While catcher Francisco Estrada and pitcher Don Rose made only brief cup-of-coffee appearances in the major leagues, the fourth man in the deal, outfielder Leroy Stanton, enjoyed moderate success with the Angels and Seattle Mariners. In 1975, the right-handed slugger batted a respectable .261 with 14 home runs and 82 RBIs. In 1977, Stanton reached his peak by hitting .275 with 27 home runs, 90 RBIs, and a .511 slugging percentage, all career highs. Those numbers, while not eye-popping, would have been more than good enough to place Stanton in the starting outfield for some bad Mets teams in the mid-1970s.

To Balk or Not to Balk

The Chicago Cubs' run of misfortune against the Mets didn't come to an end in 1969, instead carrying over to the early stages of the 1971 season. Playing a game at Shea Stadium on May 3, the Cubs and Mets found themselves tied at 2-2. In the top of the ninth inning, the Cubs rallied to load the bases with Mets relief ace Tug McGraw on the mound. As the left-handed screwballer prepared to deliver a pitch, third base umpire Stan Landes called a balk on McGraw, thereby giving the Cubs the lead. Or so it seemed. Home plate umpire Mel Steiner, to the delightful surprise of the Mets, waived off the balk. Moments before the balk took place, Steiner claimed that he had called "time out"—thus negating the balk. The Cubs, understandably upset about the timing of the call and the denial of the lead run, argued the decision, but to no avail. Given a reprieve, McGraw proceeded to pitch out of the jam and maintain the deadlock. Two innings later, Tommie Agee came off the bench and delivered a pinch-hit single, giving the Mets a controversial 3-2 win against their frustrated rivals.

Trouble for Tug

On occasion, Tug McGraw's penchant for facetious humor made him the subject of the wrath of opposing players. One such incident took place early in the 1971 season, in a series between the Mets and the eventual world champion Pittsburgh Pirates. During an April series with the Bucs, Willie Stargell belted his sixth home run of the early season against Jerry Koosman. Afterward, Tug McGraw jokingly remarked that he would throw at Stargell the next time he faced the left-handed slugger. Although McGraw was already well known for his sense of humor, Stargell did not appreciate the attempt at comedy.

"If he hits me, I'm going to kill him," Stargell vowed with a snarl. As Stargell would explain to Pittsburgh sportswriter Charley Feeney later in the season, "I'm always amazed when a pitcher becomes angry at a hitter for hitting a home run off him. When I strike out, I don't get angry at the pitcher, I get angry at myself."

Stargell simply had no patience for pitchers whom he felt had thrown at him in "retaliation" for hitting a home run—and little appreciation for the sense of humor of the wisecracking Tug McGraw.

Mourning a Manager

The death of Gil Hodges during the spring of 1972 ranks as one of the greatest tragedies in the history of the Mets. Still in his managerial prime at the age of 47, Hodges's spotless reputation likely would have kept him in place as Mets manager for several years to come. Instead, his death from a massive heart attack removed both an intelligent baseball mind and a soulful, strong-willed leader from the hierarchy of the Mets.

"[The team] started to go downhill when Gil Hodges died. He was the nearest and dearest man to my professional career," says Tom Seaver, who won 79 games and a Cy Young Award in his four years under Hodges. "It took the baseball man out of the organization's equation, and nobody else would stand up to this owner [chairman of the board M. Donald Grant]. When Gil died, things started to go downhill."

The full effects of the loss of Hodges would start to be felt in the mid-1970s, when the franchise fell into disarray at both the major league and minor league levels. Yet, there would be one last hurrah for the players left over from the Hodges regime, some of whom had participated in the 1969 world championship. Those last remnants of the Hodges era would produce a belated tribute to their fallen leader during the summer of 1973.

CHAPTER THREE

1973

Changing to Chiles

Tommie Agee's contributions to a world championship in 1969 and his popularity with New York fans could not make him a Met for life. After the 1972 season, the Mets traded an injury-prone Agee to the Houston Astros for outfielder Rich Chiles and a pitching prospect. Although the Mets might have been justified in trading a declining Agee, it remains baffling that they received so little in return for the talented center fielder. While the Mets claimed that they considered Chiles a legitimate candidate for their vacant center field position, the words of an unnamed Astros official provided far less optimism.

"He might help as a pinch-hitter," the official told *The Sporting News*, "but don't expect him to play every day."

Nonetheless, the Mets penciled in Chiles as one of six candidates to play center field, along with veterans Willie Mays and Cleon Jones, minor leaguers Don Hahn and Dave Schneck, and converted infielder Teddy Martinez. Apparently rejuvenated by the trade, a giddy Chiles reported enthusiastically to training camp. On his first day in camp, the long-haired blonde ran out to center field, jumped in the air and clicked his heels (like Ron Santo had done so annoyingly for the Cubs in 1969), and promptly fell flat on his face.

The Mets should have considered Chiles's ill-fated attempt at heel-clicking an ominous sign of things to come. Eventually realizing that he had only an average arm and no power, the Mets watched Chiles play a grand total of eight games, managing merely three hits in 25 at-bats. Not so surprisingly, Chiles found himself out of the major leagues in 1974 and 1975.

Say Hey, It's Willie Mays

While Rich Chiles was arguably the least known of the center field candidates, Willie Mays remained a household name to all generations of New York City baseball fans. Having been acquired from the San Francisco Giants in the midst of the 1972 season, the "Say Hey Kid" had played creditably for the Mets in a split role as a center fielder and first baseman. The addition of a player of Mays stature—even at an advanced age—was welcomed by the team's present-day superstar.

"All of a sudden, you've got Willie Mays playing for you. He is arguably the best player to play in the history of the game, offensively, defensively, whatever," says Tom Seaver, who had been the most recognizable Mets player prior to Mays's arrival. "[Willie] was a joy to play with. He had this boyish innocence of loving to play."

Although Mays's skills showed considerable decline by 1973, he endured as an intelligent player who did his best to help his pitchers. "When I would pitch," Seaver says, "he would come over to me. He had a list—of all the players in the [opposing]

Even at an older age, Willie Mays maintained a classical, stylish batting swing. Focus on Sport/Getty Images

lineup. He would say, 'How are you pitching him? How are you pitching to him?'"

Specifically, Mays wanted to know the types of pitches and the locations that Seaver would use against each batter so that he could position himself accordingly in center field. Mays's physical attributes of speed and power may have eroded badly by his final season, but there remained nothing wrong with his thinking approach to the game.

Center Field Soap Opera

The Mets' center field quagmire presented manager Yogi Berra with his toughest dilemma in the spring of 1973. None of the six contenders seemed like an everyday answer, not even the legendary Willie Mays, who was now a brittle 41 and no longer capable of playing the position on a daily basis. Some members of the Mets' front office believed the team might be best off by converting Cleon Jones from left field to center field, which would in turn open up the left-field slot for promising slugger John Milner (who couldn't throw at all from the outfield). The proposal left some longtime followers of the team laughing so hard that they practically came to tears. As veteran beat writer Jack Lang of the *Long Island Press* and *The Sporting News* recalled, Casey Stengel had tried Jones in center field during the mid-1960s—with disastrous results. Jones, who already faced significant challenges trying to play left field, had manned center field with all the finesse of a Brahman bull.

Thankfully, Berra had served as a coach under Stengel, which allowed him to watch Jones's stumbles in center field. An underrated evaluator of talent, Berra gave little thought to the front office's recommendation of a realigned outfield. Instead, he kept Jones in left, inserted the weak-armed Milner as the team's starting first baseman, and settled on a timeshare of Don Hahn and Mays in center. Berra's arrangement strengthened the Mets' fielding and throwing at two of their outfield positions, while leaving untouched Rusty Staub and his accurate throwing arm in right field. Without the better defensive play in the outfield, the Mets might not have squeaked out an Eastern Division title that summer.

Who Needs a Batting Coach?

In the current-day new-millennium era of baseball, every major league team employs a full-time batting coach and every organization has at least one minor league hitting instructor. Yet, such a degree of specialization was not always the case—and is actually relatively new to the "Grand Old Game." It's hard to believe, but as recently as the early 1970s, the Mets had still not employed a fulltime batting coach at any level of the organization. That finally changed in 1973, when Mets general manager Bob Scheffing hired former major league star Phil Cavarretta as the first batting instructor in the franchise's history.

Up until then, the four managers of the Mets—Casey Stengel, Wes Westrum, Gil Hodges, and Yogi Berra—had never assigned a coach to fill the duties of a hitting instructor; the managers did it themselves. With the addition of Cavarretta, that arrangement would change, but only slightly. Under the terms of his contract, Cavarretta would work with the major league hitters—but only during spring training in Florida. Once the regular season began, Cavarretta would shift his attention to the Mets' minor league system, where he would rove from affiliate to affiliate, offering his wisdom on the elusive art of hitting.

The hiring of Cavarretta represented at least some level of progressive thought within the Mets organization, but some players wondered why a full-time batting coach couldn't travel with the team throughout the season.

"They have pitching coaches on every team," said longtime Met Ed Kranepool in an interview with Mets beat writer Jack Lang, "but how many have batting coaches to help the hitters when they're in a slump?"

National League teams like the Cincinnati Reds, Los Angeles Dodgers, Pittsburgh Pirates, and St. Louis Cardinals had employed major league hitting coaches at one time or another, but the rest of the league had not yet followed suit.

Kranepool's observation, while generally accurate and insightful, struck a few longtime followers of the Mets as some-what ironic. Ten years earlier, during Kranepool's first season in the major leagues, legendary teammate Duke Snider had approached the youngster with some suggestions about his hit-ting approach. Kranepool, painfully young and rudely unrecep-tive to offers of advice, waved off the future Hall of Famer.

"You ain't doing so hot yourself," said a dismissive Kranepool, who had yet to learn the benefits of diplomacy—or a capable hitting coach.

The "Power Swing"

The presence of Phil Cavarretta wasn't the only new hitting "tool" made available to Mets batters during the spring of 1973. Youthful outfield prospect Dave Schneck, one of the competitors for the Mets' center field position, brought with him a hitting device called the "Power Swing." The contraption, which Schneck had picked up from veteran outfielder-infielder Cesar Tovar during winter ball in Venezuela, featured four plastic fins attached to a circular tube. The tube then slid neatly over the end of a bat, ready to be used by hitters taking practice swings.

Although the "Power Swing"—both the fins and the tube—weighed less than a pound, it created strong resistance when someone tried to swing a bat. If a batter swung harder, the resistance became more forceful. As a result, the "Power Swing" forced hitters to cut down their swing. The device also encouraged hitters to develop another good habit.

"It teaches you to turn the top hand over," Mets manager Yogi Berra explained to Mets beat writer Jack Lang. "It's a pretty good gimmick."

With an endorsement from a Hall of Famer like Berra, and backed up by apparently sound theory, the "Power Swing" appeared to be an effective practice tool. (It retailed for $16.95, which seemed like a reasonable price.) Yet it never achieved the mass popularity of previous inventions like the batting doughnut or the "Iron Mike" pitching machine. And it didn't help Dave Schneck, who never hit well enough to win the fulltime starting center field job.

Ladies Day

The dreaded confines of political correctness had yet to sweep the country by 1973—at least not in name—but its effects had already begun to make waves in the world of sports. Prior to the 1973 season, the Mets decided to do away with their successful "Ladies Day" promotions, in which women received discounted admission to games at Shea Stadium. The Mets made the decision largely because of pressure from the increasingly powerful women's liberation movement, which had begun to make inroads into the National Pastime. At first, the Mets considered canceling Ladies Day outright, but then gave some thought to renaming the promotion. One option that management considered was "Couples Day," in which couples received discounted tickets to certain games. The new promotion never caught on unlike the popular "Ladies Day."

The Stork

Of the 25 players who made the Mets' Opening Day roster in 1973, the biggest surprise involved the name of little-known outfielder-first baseman George Theodore. Though regarded as a prospect by the Mets' front office, Theodore seemed at least one year away from making the jump to the major leagues. And his play in the spring had seemingly done little to earn him a spot on the Mets' roster. At the time that Yogi Berra announced that he had made the team, Theodore was hitting a mere .182 in spring training exhibition games.

In trying to rationalize the decision by Berra, one particularly cruel New York writer decided to seize upon Theodore's rather awkward looks. With his beanpole build, slumped shoulders, and large wire glasses, Theodore did not exactly qualify for "heartthrob" status. The writer, perhaps only half-kiddingly, felt that Theodore's gangly appearance had helped sway Berra's decision.

"[With] any picture Yogi takes with Theodore," said the insensitive writer, "Yogi has to look like a matinee idol."

Milkshakes with "The Stork"

Whether deserving of a roster spot or not, George Theodore certainly did not fit the stereotypical appearance of a ballplayer. At six feet, four inches tall and a mere 160 pounds, the bespectacled Theodore looked more like a teenaged librarian enduring a growth spurt. Not surprisingly, his unusual appearance produced a litany of nicknames. He became most well known as "The

Stork," but others preferred "Othello," "The Masher," and one particularly bizarre moniker: "The Volga Boatsman."

According to his 1974 Topps baseball card, Theodore also had at least one inexplicable eating habit. He liked to drink marshmallow milkshakes. Yes, marshmallow. Whatever the snack or the nickname of choice, those Mets fans old enough to have experienced George Theodore will never forget him.

Felix "The Cat"

A native of Puerto Rico and one of the better middle infielders produced by the island, Felix "The Cat" Millan was a good defensive second baseman who came up with the Atlanta Braves before playing for the Mets from 1973 to 1977. Acquired (along with pitcher George Stone) in an off-season trade with the Braves, Millan became the starting second baseman on the Mets' pennant-winning team of 1973 and also earned "Met of the Year" honors from writers and broadcasters. Yet he was far better known for the unusual approach he used at the plate. Millan choked up on the bat more than any player I've ever seen—and that includes Little League—with his hands about a foot from the knob of the bat. It still amazes me that Millan never poked himself in the ribs while taking a swing with what seemed like half the bat sticking out underneath his hands. On the other hand, Millan was very hard to strike out—never more than 35 times in a single season.

Always surehanded, Felix Millan makes a two-handed catch near second base. Focus on Sport/Getty Images

Sometimes the Best Trades Are the Ones You Don't Make

The trade for Felix Millan, in which the Mets surrendered right-handed pitchers Gary Gentry and Danny Frisella, was one of the few deals that worked out favorably for Bob Scheffing as Mets general manager. Yet, the Millan trade never would have happened if some other Scheffing deals had worked out.

Prior to making the Millan trade, Scheffing offered Frisella and Gentry to the San Francisco Giants for talented center fielder Ken Henderson. Giants manager Charlie Fox reportedly turned down the offer and asked for left-handed starter Jon Matlack, whom the Mets considered untouchable. And then there was a blockbuster seven-player deal that would have sent Gentry, Frisella, Tommie Agee, and another player to the Chicago Cubs for outfielder Rick Monday, veteran right-hander Bill Hands, and a third player. Scheffing was ready to make the trade, but Cubs manager Whitey Lockman supposedly called the deal off at the last minute.

From "Iron Hands" to "The Cat"

In landing Felix Millan, who would handle second base for the next five seasons, the Mets stabilized a position that had caused almost as much consternation as their ever-chaotic third-base morass. Prior to 1973, the Mets had used 29 second basemen in 11 seasons, or an average of nearly three pivot men per year. The adventures of one of the second basemen, Chuck Hiller, epitomized the problems at the position. Hiller had such difficulty with groundballs that some observers nicknamed him "Iron Hands."

Of the 29 candidates in that span, only three had enjoyed any kind of staying power: Ron Hunt, Ken Boswell, and Al Weis. Weis earned the Babe Ruth MVP Award for his .455 batting average and Game 5 home run in the 1969 World Series, but otherwise failed to hit much as a platoon second baseman for the Mets. And even Hunt and Boswell had their problems, considering that they both lacked the ideal amount of range needed for the position.

In 1964, Hunt's hitting earned him a place on the National League All-Star team, but the Mets remained unsatisfied with his defensive play. Later that season, the Mets moved Hunt to third base to make room for a young second baseman named Bobby Klaus. Hunt, a fiery sort who had both a temper and little use for diplomacy, didn't handle the transition with delicacy.

"Let them move *him* to third base," Hunt said angrily in referring to the newcomer, Klaus. "He ain't made the All-Star team yet, has he?"

Now that Klaus had been made fully welcome, he proceeded to hit a punchless .244 in 56 games. He fared even worse the following season, hitting a meager .191 in 288 at-bats, in what amounted to his major league swansong. Hunt turned out to be right after all; Klaus was certainly no All-Star—and wouldn't be one in the future, either.

Fregosi's Flop

Sometimes you just have to admit to making a mistake. That's exactly what the Mets did on July 11, 1973, when they sent one of their grand failures, veteran infielder Jim Fregosi, to the Texas Rangers for a pile of cash. With Fregosi now returned to the American League, the Mets had no players—and only a small amount of money—to show for their ill-fated trade of Nolan Ryan to the California Angels after the 1971 season.

Fregosi's year-and-a-half tenure in New York had evolved into nothing short of disaster. After failing to settle the team's longstanding third base problem in 1972, Fregosi's game had continued to plummet in 1973. With a .234 batting average in 45 games, Fregosi had lost his position to left-handed hitting Wayne Garrett. Although only 31 years old at the time, Fregosi would never again regain the All-Star form he had once shown as a member of the Angels. Some critics attributed Fregosi's unusually early decline as a player to his hard-drinking style, which added to problems with his expanding waistline. New York City, with its 24-hour nightlife, only exacerbated Fregosi's penchant for late hours and barhopping.

First Half Follies

The Mets played so badly over the first half of the 1973 season that rumors abounded over the possible firing of Yogi Berra. One rumor had the Mets tossing Berra, who was frequently second-guessed by the New York media, and replacing him with Billy Martin, who was about to be dumped by the Detroit Tigers. The Mets' front office laughed off the report, which turned out to be more dime-store gossip than legitimate journalism.

Still, the struggles of the Mets prompted the *New York Post* to run a readers poll in mid-July. Seeking to place blame on the appropriate individuals, the newspaper poll asked a simple question: Who should go: Berra, Chairman of the Board M. Donald Grant, or general manager Bob Scheffing?

The results of the poll showed that Mets fans held Berra the *least* responsible of the three men in command. Of the 4,000 ballots cast, only 611 felt that Berra should be fired. In contrast, just

Although an All-Star with the Angels, Jim Fregosi flopped badly in trying to make the transition to third base for the Mets.
Focus on Sport/Getty Images

over 1,200 fans felt that Grant should be given the heave-ho. Yet, the fans who responded seemed to think that Scheffing, with his questionable track record of making trades, should be held most responsible for the Mets' malaise. Scheffing received a total of 1,448 "fire him" votes, putting him first in a poll in which he would have preferred to have finished last.

Ya Gotta Believe

Tug McGraw could be tough to interview because he liked to joke about *everything* and sometimes wouldn't give you a sincere answer to the most serious of questions. Yet, there was something inherently noble about McGraw. Nearly two decades after he retired as a player, McGraw refused to allow inoperable brain cancer to deter his ever-present enthusiasm and spirit. He allowed no bitterness or self-pity during his ill-fated battle, to which he succumbed in January of 2004. It's not that well-known, but the Mets actually thought McGraw had become afflicted with cancer as far back as 1974, which partly motivated their decision to trade him to the Philadelphia Phillies. McGraw had developed a growth on his back, which worried the Mets so much that they rushed into making a trade (for catcher John Stearns, outfielder Del Unser, and left-handed pitcher Mac Scarce) that they would later regret. As it turned out, doctors determined that McGraw's growth was not cancerous, which left the Phillies with a healthy fireman for the balance of the 1970s and beyond.

No one seems to know for sure how sincere McGraw was in sounding his "Ya Gotta Believe" motto throughout the 1973 season. McGraw had initially picked up the saying from a pair of nuns, who were offering the ace reliever hope that the Mets could turn around their fortunes and re-enter the pennant race.

McGraw started using the slogan a few weeks later on July 9, right after team chairman M. Donald Grant chided his last-place players in a pregame clubhouse meeting at Shea Stadium, insisting they could win if only they "believed" in themselves. (Grant, a sentimental sort, was prone to such rah-rah meetings, which often had players giggling by the end of the sermon.) At the end of Grant's sappy address, McGraw proceeded to yell "Ya Gotta Believe" over and over while hysterically jumping up and down. The new slogan seemed to pay immediate dividends, as the Mets went out and posted a 2-1 victory in 12 innings on Felix Millan's RBI single.

Grant considered McGraw's actions mocking in nature, but the left-hander kept up the "act" for the rest of the season, convincing the team's beat writers that he meant what he said. So what may have started out as a gesture of sarcasm actually became a rallying cry for an under-talented but overachieving Mets team.

Second Half Surge

The Mets' turnaround in 1973 has never received as much publicity as the comeback of 1969, but it ranks almost as impressively given the distance in the standings. As of June 25, the injury-racked, bullpen-plagued Mets found themselves in last place in a mediocre National League East. Nearly two months later, on August 20, the Mets still remained stuck in the quicksand of last place—with no end to the misery in sight.

In late August, the Mets began a torrential surge that marked the highlight of their Jekyll-and-Hyde season. The Mets would win 21 of their last 29 overall, including a sparkling record of 19-8 in September. On September 21, the Mets finally reached the pinnacle of the Eastern Division with a 10-2 throttling of the Pittsburgh Pirates. Although the victory put New York's record at

The spirit of the 1973 Mets—Tug McGraw. Focus on Sport/Getty Images

exactly 77-77—the high point of mediocrity—the Mets had managed to slip past the Pirates into first place. The Mets remained in the top spot for the rest of the season, claiming the division with a mediocre mark of 82-79—the worst record ever by a team to reach the postseason.

So why did the Mets play so much better the final six weeks after playing so poorly for nearly five months? First-half injuries had placed frontline talents like Jerry Grote, John Milner, Buddy Harrelson, Cleon Jones, and Willie Mays on the disabled list at one time or another. The bullpen also underachieved badly, as relief ace Tug McGraw posted an ERA of 6.17 through games of July 17.

By August, most of the injured Met regulars had returned to the lineup. In addition, the performance of three Mets in particular helped the team overcome its bumbling start. From mid-July through the end of the season, McGraw pitched to the tune of a 1.62 ERA. During a personal 13-game stretch in September, an unyielding McGraw notched nine saves and three wins. Another Mets veteran, left fielder Cleon Jones, recovered from problems with his chronically sore and "tired" feet to hit six home runs over the final two weeks of the regular season. And then there was young third baseman Wayne Garrett, who made everyone forget Jim Fregosi by hitting .315 with six home runs and 22 runs scored during the critical run in September.

Yogi and Cleon

Hall of Fame sportswriter Dick Young pinpointed the Mets' 1973 turnaround even more specifically, citing a relatively little-known meeting between manager Yogi Berra and a sulking Cleon Jones in mid-August. In the midst of a West Coast trip, Berra paid a visit to Jones's room in a San Diego hotel. With players and coaches grumbling about Jones's casual style of play and a seeming unwillingness to play with what he called "tired feet," Berra felt a face-to-face meeting was necessary. According to Young, the conversation included a heart-felt plea from Berra to Jones. "The team needs you, and I need you," Berra said firmly but without anger. Cracking a smile, Berra then offered a half-kidding follow-up: "What are you trying to do, get me fired?"

After the meeting, Jones started to hit, culminating in his two-week reign of terror against National League pitchers at the end of the regular season. With Jones playing more like his primetime version of 1969, the Mets finally salted away the muddled Eastern Division pennant race.

The Playoff Brawl

The fracas involving Buddy Harrelson and Pete Rose remains the indelible moment of the 1973 National League Championship Series between the Mets and the Cincinnati Reds. With the Mets leading Game 3, 9-2, Rose attempted to break up a double play by sliding hard into Harrelson at second base. The rough slide failed to stop the Mets from turning two, but succeeded in angering Harrelson, who felt that Rose had thrown his elbow at him. Harrelson, all 150 pounds of him, then shoved Rose, leading to a barrage of pushing and shoving between the two men. Both benches and bullpens emptied, resulting in one of the most memorable playoff brawls of all time.

Within a few moments, Rose was pulled out of the middle of the melee by Johnny Bench. In the meantime, other players scuffled, particularly the Mets' Buzz Capra and the Reds' Pedro Borbon. The two pitchers exchanged a throw of fists before their dispute was also brought to an end. By the time that both teams had settled down and returned to their corners, the umpires decided that no one merited an ejection—not even Harrelson and Rose; National League president Chub Feeney reasoned that he didn't want to see players ejected from such an important play-off game. (Harrelson and Rose were later fined, each hit with a not-so-lofty penalty of $250.) Then, in the bottom half of the sixth inning, Rose returned to his fielding post in left field, where he promptly incurred a barrage of debris thrown by some angry fans in the bleachers.

For future Mets broadcaster Howie Rose, who was watching the game as a fan at Shea Stadium that day, the involvement of the fans in the aftermath of the incident became the bigger story.

"The most frightening aspect of that to me was not the brawl," says Rose (no relation to Pete), "but it was the reaction of the fans necessitating that Cleon Jones, Tom Seaver, Willie Mays, Yogi Berra, and Rusty Staub walk out to left field to motion to the fans to cool it. There was a considerable threat of the Mets forfeiting the game if that stuff continued."

Not wanting to award the Reds a forfeit win in the playoffs and fearful over Pete Rose's safety, the umpires had wisely asked Berra and Mays to plead with the fans in left field. Joined by Jones, Staub, and Seaver, the five-man contingent made its way to left field and implored the fans to stop their unruly efforts in pelting Rose with garbage. The fans complied, enabling Rose to finish the game in relative peace and allowing the Mets to finish off their 9-2 drubbing of the Reds.

The next day, Mets chairman M. Donald Grant asked both Harrelson and Pete Rose to meet at home plate prior to Game 5, as a way of showing that the players had disposed of any hard feelings. Harrelson agreed to the summit meeting, but Rose rejected the invitation.

"That wouldn't look good," said "Charley Hustle," who might be the last person in baseball to know what looks good.

CHAPTER FOUR

The Rest of the 1970s

Benny and the Mets

Some players come to symbolize an era in a franchise's history. Just as Horace Clarke became the signature player for the Yankees of the late 1960s and early 1970s, the name of Benny Ayala strikes a chord with Mets fans recalling the inglorious days of the mid-1970s. Perhaps it has something to do with the name; how can you not remember a guy named Benny Ayala? Or perhaps it has more to do with Ayala's mediocrity as a Met (though he did have a decent stint as a platoon player with the Baltimore Orioles). Or maybe it relates to a career that started so promisingly only to reach a level of nothing more than journeyman status. In the case of Ayala, few have begun their careers in grander fashion. Making his debut on August 27, 1974, at Shea Stadium, the native of Puerto Rico promptly homered against Houston's Tom Griffin in his first major league at-bat. The right-handed hitting outfielder thus became the first National Leaguer to homer in his inaugural at-bat in 13 years, dating back to the pre-Mets era. Making the home run even more dramatic, Ayala's blast helped lift the Mets to a 4-2 victory over the Astros.

The Game That Wouldn't Die

Over the years, the National League and American League have come to differ on a number of rules, most prominently the designated hitter. A lesser-known difference involves the curfew. For years, American League rules stipulated that no inning could begin after one o'clock in the morning local time, while the National League provided no allowances for a curfew; a game could theoretically stretch into the following afternoon, if need be. During the latter stages of the 1974 season, the Mets probably wished there had been a curfew.

On the evening of September 11, the Mets began their game with the Cardinals at 8:00 p.m. The following morning, at the hour of 3:13, they concluded their marathon at Shea Stadium. Within the span of seven hours and four minutes, the Mets and Cards played 25 innings of baseball, with St. Louis emerging as 4-3 victors. A Mets loss was excruciating enough; the way in which they lost only made it all the more insufferable. In the top of the 25th, Cardinals speedster Bake McBride reached first base against Mets right-hander Hank Webb. Rightly considering McBride a base-stealing threat, Webb tried to pick him off—only to throw the ball past first base. Webb threw the ball so wildly that McBride went to third base and then scored on an error by Mets catcher Ron Hodges—giving the Cardinals what would prove to be the game-winning run.

The Mets and Cardinals combined to use a whopping 50 players, including 13 pitchers. The number of players nearly matched the number of fans left standing at the end. Of the 13,460 fans who attended the game, only about 1,500 remained throughout the late night and early morning hours to witness the game to its conclusion. The fans should have been rewarded with medals; instead they had to endure another defeat during a lost season.

Piggy, Aaron, and Oh

Joe Pignatano, who served the Mets as their longtime bullpen coach under a variety of different managers, was probably best known for growing tomatoes and other vegetables in the home bullpen at Shea Stadium.

In the winter of 1974, Pignatano achieved another—albeit less publicized—"claim to fame" when he became involved in one of baseball's most historic home-run hitting contests. With Korakuen Stadium in Japan providing the backdrop on November 2, "Piggy" was given the honor of serving as the "designated pitcher" in the head-to-head home-run derby featuring the Braves' Hank Aaron and Tokyo Giants legend Sadaharu Oh. With Aaron recently having overtaken Babe Ruth as the major leagues' all-time home-run king, the contest pitted the American home-run king against the Japanese leader in home runs. Hitting against the batting practice pitches of Pignatano, Aaron won the competition, with 10 home runs to Oh's nine.

The Fans Know Best

Some trades produce an unpopular reaction—and then just get worse. Such was the case with the deal the Mets made after the 1974 season, when they swapped the team's heartbeat—reliever Tug McGraw—and outfielders Don Hahn and Dave Schneck to the Philadelphia Phillies for catcher John Stearns, outfielder Del Unser, and left-handed pitcher Mac Scarce. The majority of Mets fans hated the trade as soon as it was announced, given the loss of the beloved McGraw and the absence of brand-name talent coming in return. The Mets' brass tried to justify the deal by pointing out that Unser would fill an immediate need in center field and that Stearns, a top-notch prospect, would become the team's catcher of the future. Well, Stearns did become the Mets' No. 1 receiver by 1977, and earned notoriety as one of baseball's fastest catchers (setting a National League record for most steals by a catcher in 1978), but never developed into the all-round star the Mets had anticipated. As for Unser, he did enjoy a long career as a reliable pinch-hitter, but failed miserably as an everyday player with the Mets. More significantly, he became the symbol for a trade that should never have been made—while also becoming the frequent object of New Yorkers' collective scorn.

The Decline and Fall
of Cleon Jones

At the peak of his career, Cleon Jones vied for the National League batting title and emerged as one of the most integral members of the 1969 "Miracle Mets." At the low points, Jones sometimes angered teammates and managers with what appeared to be lackadaisical play in the outfield and on the base paths. In hitting rock bottom, he encountered trouble with the law and became an embarrassment to the Mets organization.

During the spring of 1975, St. Petersburg police discovered a naked Jones sleeping in the back of a van with a 21-year-old woman, who was also without clothing. The woman happened to be holding narcotics, which only added to Jones's level of embar-

Though perhaps best remembered for catching the last out of the 1969 World Series, it was at the plate where Cleon Jones starred most of the time. Focus on Sport/Getty Images

rassment. When the police asked Jones—a married man, no less—to identify himself, he responded that he was "C. Joseph Jones, a laborer."

The police arrested Jones on charges of indecent exposure, but later dropped the charges because of a lack of evidence. Still, the incident left Jones's reputation tarnished and motivated Mets chairman M. Donald Grant to levy a fine of $2,000 for "betraying the image of the club." To make matters worse, Grant called a news conference of circus-like proportions, forcing Jones to issue a humiliating public apology.

The Jones saga only worsened during the 1975 season. On July 18, manager Yogi Berra inserted Jones into a game as a pinch-hitter. After the at-bat, Berra told Jones to stay in the game and take his position in left field. Jones refused, instead walking away from his manager. The act of insubordination, coupled with the spring training van incident, brought Jones's career as a Met to an end. Once a hero of the 1969 Mets, Jones was given his unconditional release.

Later in the season, the rival Yankees offered Jones a two-year contract, but the veteran outfielder curiously turned down the offer, citing the lack of a signing bonus as part of the deal. The following season, Jones signed a contract with the Chicago White Sox, but he lasted only a handful of games in the Windy City, bringing his career to an unceremonious end.

Twin Killing Times Four

Joe Torre's strengths as a player included his lethal bat—which helped him win the 1971 National League batting championship and MVP Award—and the versatility to play as a catcher, third baseman, and first baseman. His main weakness involved his lack of speed, which made him one of the slowest base runners of his era. Torre's problems with foot speed were never more apparent than on July 21, 1975, when the Mets played the Astros.

Torre came to bat four times that night, each time with Felix Millan on first base. Millan should not have bothered reaching base, because the result of Torre's at-bats was the same each time: Torre grounded into a double play four consecutive times, accounting for eight of the Mets' 27 outs on offense. Torre's quartet of "double dips" tied a major league record originally set by Hall of Famer Goose Goslin in 1934 and then matched by Mike Kreevich in 1939.

Not surprisingly, the Mets lost the game, 6-2, to the Astros. The Mets scored their only runs on home runs by Rusty Staub and Dave Kingman, but in this case, four of a kind did far more damage than a pair of aces.

On Second Thought …

On the surface, Joe Torre's first managerial tenure in New York appeared to be a failure. With little talent at his disposal, Torre's Mets won few games. While the manager took more than his fair share of criticism from the New York media, some of his players realized what the Mets had in Torre. The manager's supporters included a thinking-man's player like Tom Seaver, who had previously played against and with Torre before playing *for* him.

"One of the nicest guys you'll ever want to meet," says Seaver. "There was a window of time when somebody said to me, 'You'll be a general manager one day.' Well, the first person I would have called to run my ball club would have been Joe Torre. From an ethical standpoint, no BS. What you see is what you get. You get a straight line from him. You don't get a line delivered to you with some ulterior motive. He's just as straight up as you can be."

Given his honesty, loyalty, and general decency, Torre's success with the *other* New York team comes as no surprise to Seaver.

Multiple Milestones for Tom Terrific

It's not often that a pitcher records a shutout and two other major milestones on the same day. Yet, that's what happened on September 1, 1975, when Tom Seaver pitched one of his typically masterful games at Shea Stadium. Facing the hard-hitting lineup of the Pittsburgh Pirates, Seaver achieved his first milestone when he struck out Manny Sanguillen in the seventh inning. The strikeout gave him 200 for the season, making him the first pitcher in big league history to accumulate eight consecutive 200-strikeout seasons. (Seaver would pile up another 200 strikeout season in 1976, extending the streak to nine years.) Pitching masterfully, Seaver blanked Pittsburgh that day, finishing the hallmark game with 10 strikeouts. The victory put him at an even 20 wins for the season. It marked the fourth time he had reached the milestone in his Hall of Fame career. Seaver went on to win his third Cy Young Award; only Sandy Koufax had reached that number previously.

Danny Frisella

There is no greater tragedy in major league baseball than the death of a player during the youthful prime of his career. The Mets family felt that tragedy on the first day of 1977, when the franchise lost a former teammate affectionately known as "Bear."

Although he was with the Milwaukee Brewers at the time of his death, Danny Frisella will always be remembered as a member of the Mets. On New Year's Day, 1977, the fun-loving Frisella was riding a dune buggy near Phoenix, Arizona, when the vehicle suddenly overturned. As the dune buggy toppled over, Frisella's head collided with the ground, causing severe and irreversible damage. The hard-throwing right-hander was only 30 years old.

If not for the emergence of Tug McGraw, Frisella might have risen to the top of the Mets bullpen and might have become one of the game's dominant relief aces of the early 1970s. Blessed with a high-riding fastball and a rubber arm, Frisella proved an excellent complement to McGraw as the Mets' top right-hander out of the bullpen from 1970 through much of 1972. After he struggled in the second half of 1972, the pitching-rich Mets considered Frisella expendable and dealt him and starter Gary Gentry to the Braves for a much-needed second baseman in Felix Millan.

The news of Frisella's death hit hard with his former teammates, including his former roommate Rod Gaspar.

"We had just moved to Mission Viejo when I heard that story," says Gaspar, who played with Frisella in 1969 and 1970. "He was a friend of mine, and I knew his fiancée, who later became his wife. He was a great guy. We had a lot of fun together. Good guy. Danny was a good guy; I enjoyed him very much. It was through him … how I met my wife, Sheridan. That was 35 years ago. He was my buddy."

Although he pitched only a handful of seasons in New York, Frisella became popular with teammates like Gaspar. He was also a funny, responsible, and devoted father and husband.

"Life was just too short with him," says Pam Frisella, Danny's widow, "but three months after he died, Daniel Vincent, Jr. was born on what would have been Danny's 31st birthday. I saw the same set of eyes to keep an eye on me. Even though Daniel has never met his dad, he has the same walk and identical personality as his dad."

Rest in peace, Bear.

A Bitter Day at Shea

The Mets had made some horrific trades in their first 15 years of existence, but the two worst—Amos Otis for Joe Foy, and Nolan Ryan for Jim Fregosi—involved giving up future stars who had struggled at the major league level. When "The Franchise" was traded, Mets fans knew all too well what the front office was giving away.

Writers referred to it as the "Midnight Massacre." On June 15, 1977, just hours before the midnight trading deadline, the Mets shipped Tom Seaver to the Cincinnati Reds for a package of four players. Such a trade, at one time considered unthinkable, stemmed from a nasty dispute between the ace pitcher and a key member of Mets management, a man whom Seaver considered unjust in his dealings with players.

"My welcome mat ran out with a guy that I worked for named M. Donald Grant," says Seaver, referring to the Mets' chairman of the board. "He didn't like me and I didn't like him. One day he called me a communist. And I wish I was kidding you, but he was a guy who had a real plantation mentality. And I stuck up for the players and I stuck up for myself, and he didn't like it. He traded me to Cincinnati. I hated to go. I hated to leave."

Mets fans hated the trade even more than Seaver. A lasting symbol of both the 1969 world championship team and the 1973 National League pennant-winners, Seaver had become the most popular player in the history of the team. As if the loss of Seaver wasn't horrific enough, Mets fans were certainly not appeased upon hearing the names of the four players that would come to New York as compensation for "Tom Terrific." Of the four, only two had major league experience and neither possessed any kind of marquee value: pitcher Pat Zachry and second baseman Doug Flynn. While Zachry had shared National Rookie of the Year honors in 1976, he certainly didn't appear to have the kind of talent that would make him a No. 1 starter, something the Mets needed given the departure of Seaver. In the meantime, Flynn appeared to be one-dimensional: a smooth-fielding, light-hitting second baseman who also lacked star potential. And then there were the two minor leaguers the Mets received: outfielders Steve Henderson and Dan Norman. Both were deemed good prospects, but neither had the stamp of "can't miss" attached to his resume.

As many Mets fans might have predicted, the deal turned out to be a virtual disaster. Seaver remained an effective pitcher for Cincinnati, pitching a no-hitter in 1978 (an achievement that somehow eluded him with the Mets), and helping the Reds to the Western Division title in 1979. As for the package of four players the Mets received, none achieved anything more than mediocrity as major leaguers, and even in combination, they failed to come close to matching the impact of Seaver. Zachry worked as both a starter and reliever, becoming a decent utility pitcher but nothing more. As expected, Flynn defined the stereotype of a no-hit, good-field middle infielder, a far cry from the days of Felix Millan. Henderson became a singles-hitting outfielder, best suited to platoon duty, or better yet, a bench role. And Norman completely failed to pan out, making only brief pit stops in the major leagues.

On some occasions, trading a veteran star for a package of younger players works out, expediting the rebuilding process. For the Mets, all it did was extend the phase of reconstruction while denying fans the pleasure of watching "The Franchise" pitch for them.

Two More Trades

The date of June 15, 1977, remains the most active trading day in Mets history. In addition to the dumping of Tom Seaver, the Mets made two other significant trades that day in anticipation of the midnight trading deadline. Frustrated with the frequent strikeouts, periodic defensive lapses, and the temperamental nature of slugging first baseman Dave Kingman, the Mets traded "King Kong" to the San Diego Padres for infielder (and future manager) Bobby Valentine and pitcher Paul Siebert. Neither had an impact while playing for the Mets, except for Valentine's frequent second-guessing of manager Joe Torre (according to one reporter who covered the team in the 1970s). In a less-publicized deal, the Mets also acquired versatile infielder-outfielder Joel Youngblood from the St. Louis Cardinals for light-hitting shortstop Mike Phillips. Of the three trades, this one turned out the best, as Youngblood became a serviceable utility player and part-time starter. Yet the trade did little to erase the memory of losing Seaver, who would become the first player enshrined in Cooperstown with the logo of the Mets engraved on his Hall of Fame plaque.

Seaver for Sutton

According to research unearthed by baseball historian Bill Deane, the Mets almost traded Tom Seaver earlier in the decade. During the spring of 1976, the Mets and Los Angeles Dodgers entertained serious trade discussions. The prospective blockbuster trade would have sent Seaver to the Dodgers for another future Hall of Famer, Don Sutton.

When news of the nearly completed trade became public, Mets fans reacted with outrage. They wanted no part of a trade that would have disposed of their favored son and pitching superstar. As a result of the hue and cry, Mets management decided to call off the trade talks with the Dodgers.

In retrospect, Mets fans probably would have preferred the trade with the Dodgers. That way, the Mets would have received a standout pitcher like Sutton—who remained an effective pitcher through 1986—rather than the four mediocrities that arrived from Cincinnati.

Montanez' Revenge

A review of Mets history produces a mix of bad trades (Amos Otis, Nolan Ryan, Tug McGraw, and Tom Seaver) and good ones (Gary Carter and Keith Hernandez). There have also been some unusual deals.

On December 8, 1977, the Mets made one of their strangest trades ever: an odd four-team, 11-player deal with the Texas Rangers, Pittsburgh Pirates, and Atlanta Braves. In their part of the deal, the Mets surrendered first baseman John Milner and left-handed starter Jon Matlack while acquiring only first baseman Willie Montanez and journeyman outfielders Tom Grieve and Ken Henderson in return. On the surface, Milner for Montanez seemed like a fairly even swap (with a slight edge to Montanez), leaving the other part of the deal as Matlack for Grieve and Henderson. How could the Mets front office have considered two mediocre outfielders fair compensation for a quality left-handed starting pitcher like Matlack? The reasoning behind the trade remains a mystery, but the deal did produce one of the most colorful players the franchise has ever seen. Let's consider just a few characteristics that made Montanez one of the most stylish showboats in Mets history and even prompted one Shea Stadium hawker to shout: "Here, y'ar, get your Willie Montanez hot dogs!"

1) In the field, Montanez caught pop-ups with one hand and then snapped his glove downward with an overhand swipe, producing a kind of "snatch catch" that Rickey Henderson later made famous. Montanez used a similar style on groundballs, seemingly slapping at the ball with his mitt as he snared choppers and grounders.

2) When holding runners at first base, Montanez sometimes slapped base runners on the backside *without* the ball, hoping to

distract the runner into coming off the base. The stunt so angered the Atlanta Braves and base runner Vic Correll that the National League fined Montanez for what was considered an unsportsmanlike maneuver.

3) At times, Montanez issued warnings to base runners that he felt slid too aggressively into first base. While playing for the Braves, Montanez held on Mets base runner Lenny Randle at first base. As Randle led off the bag, Montanez mumbled, "Gonna break fingers." Unsure about what had been said, Randle responded, "What?" Montanez repeated the line, this time more slowly and clearly. "Gonna break your fingers." Afraid that Montanez meant what he said and unwilling to take a chance that he didn't, Randle proceeded to take off for second base on the next pitch.

4) Montanez also had several unusual habits that he displayed as a batsman. Whenever he walked into the batter's box, Montanez flipped his bat from end to end, skillfully catching it with his hand. He repeated the "flip" when he swung at a pitch and failed to put it in play.

5) After drawing a walk, Montanez did exactly that—he *walked* to first base. The habit made him the antithesis of Pete Rose, who always sprinted to first after being issued a base on balls.

6) Montanez became best known for his home-run trot, which he first started experimenting with during his rookie season with the Philadelphia Phillies and then refined while playing winter ball in his native Puerto Rico. If Montanez hit a ball that he knew would reach home-run distance, he would remain standing at home plate for several seconds, admiring the drive as it made its way beyond the outfield walls. After Montanez finally started running, he would approach first base by shuffling his feet and then jumping, landing squarely on the base with both

feet. He repeated the "pitter patter" steps at each base, but changed his routine in preparing to arrive at home plate. As he approached the plate, Montanez stopped jogging and slowly walked the final few feet. He then stepped squarely on the middle of the plate, punctuating a home run trot that became known as "Montanez' Revenge," and further aggravating an already irritated pitcher. (Veteran right-hander Gene Garber once threatened Montanez with a bean ball if he ever embarked on "Montanez' Revenge" against him. Fortunately, Montanez never homered against the former Phillies and Braves reliever.)

Montanez' stylish flair established himself as the king of major league hot dogs. As former San Francisco Giants teammate Tito Fuentes, a resplendent player in his own right, conceded in an interview with *The New York Times:* "[Willie] is the No. 1 hot dog in baseball. He is No. 1, and I am No. 2."

Although Montanez' hot dog tendencies disgusted some of his opponents, Mets manager Joe Torre welcomed him with open arms in the spring of 1978. Torre, who admitted that he once despised Montanez' antics as an opposing player, had come to appreciate the veteran first baseman for his ability to play every day, his eagerness to play hard, and his rock-solid steadiness as a run-producing, slick-fielding first baseman.

Montanez' performance eventually won over the New York press, including its crustiest members. Longtime New York sportswriter Dick Young provided this balanced, on-the-money portrayal of Montanez in the July 8, 1978 edition of *The Sporting News:*

"Willie Montanez is such a hot dog that it takes a quart of mustard to cover him," wrote Young, "but when a hot dog produces he is called colorful. Montanez gets $300,000 a year, the most ever paid to a Met, but at the rate he is knocking in runs, he is underpaid in the present market."

With little talent around him in New York, Montanez immediately became one of the best players on the team, but didn't act like a prima donna in the clubhouse or in the dugout.

"He came in as one of the guys," said catcher John Stearns, who didn't always appreciate showboating players. "He didn't come in as anybody special."

While maintaining a refreshingly level mindset, Montanez emerged as the team's premier offensive power threat in 1978, hitting a team-high 17 home runs with a team-leading 96 RBIs.

Monty and Bobby V.

Willie Montanez' antics in rounding the bases indirectly resulted in a bit of trouble for one of his teammates. Bobby Valentine, a journeyman infielder and outfielder long before he became a controversial manager, came up with the idea to imitate Montanez' actions. After hitting a rare four-bagger in a 1978 game, Valentine mimicked Montanez' home run trot as he circled the bases. The team's Kangaroo Court—a mock court that imposed fines against players for boneheaded plays and other minor transgressions—slapped Valentine with a fine for his "homage" to Montanez. (Good thing for Bobby V. it was his only home run of the season.) Given such offbeat behavior by the future Mets manager, it should have surprised few when Valentine was ejected from a game many years later, only to return to the dugout wearing a fake mustache and darkened glasses.

Montanez' Revenge No More

Unfortunately, Willie Montanez' stock did not remain high as a member of the Mets. After a productive debut in New York, Montanez found himself bogged in a deep slump at the beginning of the 1979 season. New York fans, who seemed to accept his on-field histrionics the previous summer as he racked up RBIs, turned into boo-birds when Montanez came to the plate or made an error in the field.

By August, the combined effects of Montanez' confused flailing at the plate and the increasing ire of the fans resulted in his departure; the Mets traded him to the Rangers for two players to be named later (which turned out to be pitcher Ed Lynch and former Met first baseman Mike Jorgensen). "Montanez' Revenge" would no longer be a regular occurrence at Shea Stadium.

Saying Goodbye to Kooz

Just how bad were the Mets in 1978? Their longtime starter, Jerry Koosman, posted a not-so-terrible ERA of 3.75, but managed to win only three of 18 decisions. That's what happens when the eight players on the field beside you provide little in the way of offensive or defensive support. This season followed a 20-loss campaign with a 3.49 ERA in 1977. How quickly and completely had things changed at Shea? Koosman had won 21 games in 1976.

Given Koosman's advancing age and the need for young talent everywhere, the Mets decided to trade the veteran left-hander, who had pitched all 12 of his seasons in New York, during the coming winter. On December 8, the Mets dealt "Kooz" to the

Minnesota Twins for two young pitchers: Greg Field and Jesse Orosco.

No one realized it at the time, but the Mets were actually trading a symbol of their 1969 championship for a symbol of a future title. In 1986, Orosco would record the final out of the World Series, just as Koosman did in clinching the team's only other world championship in 1969.

I Don't Love New York

In their continuing search for left-handed power in the late 1970s, the Mets hoped they had found—at long last—an appropriate solution.

On March 27, 1979, the Mets traded promising right-hander Nino Espinosa to the Philadelphia Phillies for infielder Jose Moreno and first baseman-third baseman Richie Hebner. Given his reputation as a hard-nosed player and his experience playing for both a world championship team in Pittsburgh and a playoff team in Philadelphia, the Mets believed (rather foolishly, as it turned out) that Hebner would fill their long troublesome third base position.

Although Hebner possessed a winning pedigree, the Mets should have realized that his personality did not fit the demands of New York City.

"He just never wanted to play in New York, he defied the Mets to obtain him in a trade," says Mets broadcaster and analyst Howie Rose. "They did trade for him, he came here, and was absolutely miserable—and played like it."

Unfortunately but predictably, Hebner's stay in the Big Apple soon turned into a disaster. New York fans booed Hebner as he struggled both at the plate and in re-adjusting to playing third base (after having been shifted to first base by the Phillies).

Just a few days before Hebner's wedding day, the Mets admitted to their mistake and tried to cut their losses. They sent Hebner to the Detroit Tigers for a pair of mediocre players, outfielder Jerry Morales and third baseman Phil Mankowski. Mets general manager Joe McDonald had come to the realization that the New York lifestyle simply did not suit Hebner.

"Richie hated crowds and traffic," McDonald told *The Sporting News* in November of 1979. "He went into Manhattan only once all the time he was here."

And as it turned out, Hebner came to dread his regular appearances in Queens, too.

Misery for Maddox

Like many of the Mets of the late 1970s, Elliott Maddox' memories of those inglorious seasons are something other than warm. Maddox had played at Shea Stadium as a member of the Yankees when the two teams shared the Queens facility in the mid-1970s. It was in that same outfield that Maddox badly injured his knee on a wet June day in 1975.

Still, when Maddox first joined the Mets in 1978, he viewed the move as a welcome homecoming—an opportunity to return to his roots in the Metropolitan area. In contrast to Richie Hebner, Maddox reinforced his love of the city by becoming the only Met to live in Manhattan; most of the other players lived in the suburbs of Westchester County or in New Jersey.

Unfortunately, Maddox did not feel a similar bond with the Mets as he felt toward the surrounding community.

"The Mets' front office at that time—that was probably the craziest story of all," Maddox says of his days with the Mets. "When I came in, you had M. Donald Grant [the chairman] and Joe McDonald [the general manager], and then in 1980 [Fred]

Wilpon and [Nelson] Doubleday took over, with 'Mr. Bow-Tie' [Frank Cashen, the general manager]."

Dealing with the front office became a chore for Maddox.

"Boy," Maddox says with a gasp, "you didn't really *deal* with them. It was survival of the fittest. They didn't really know what they were doing. Especially that first group."

Grant and McDonald reported to president and team owner Linda de Roulet, who knew little about baseball. "That was Joan Payson's daughter," Maddox says. "Wonderful woman. But being the owner of a baseball team wasn't what she should have been doing."

No Place for a Baby

Given his struggles and the team's general failures, Elliott Maddox would have liked nothing better than a trade away from the Mets. It almost happened, but the deal was canceled for one of the strangest reasons in baseball history.

"I remember there was a trade between the Mets and the California Angels," Maddox recalls. "Dickie Thon was being traded from the Angels to the Mets, and I was going to the Angels. And it was announced. I knew about it. And I was in a state of euphoria. Then, [team owner] Mrs. de Roulet canceled the trade; she reneged on it. She saw a picture of Dickie Thon and said, 'Oh, he's just a baby. Oh, he's just a baby. We can't make this trade. He's just a baby. How can he play major league base-ball?' That's how it worked. No deal. It was cancelled. That trade went from being announced [to nothing]. Because he looked like a baby."

The Third Call is the One That Counts

Over the years, the Mets have been involved in some weird umpiring decisions, some of which have directly affected outcomes of games. One that did not—but might rank as the strangest call—occurred in the midst of the dreary 1979 season. Not surprisingly, the controversy involved a crew of replacement umpires working in place of striking arbiters.

On April 24, the Mets played host to the San Francisco Giants. With Richie Hebner on first base and Frank Taveras on third in the bottom of the first inning, Lee Mazzilli delivered a fly ball to the outfield. Jack Clark caught the ball with ease, but in the course of attempting to make a throw, he dropped the ball. Taveras, who had properly tagged up at third base, scored easily. Yet, the Mets' other base runner, the unfortunate Mr. Hebner, had more difficulty. Upon noticing that Clark had dropped the ball, Hebner tried to advance to second base, only to be tagged out by Bill "Mad Dog" Madlock. (In some ways, the play epitomized Hebner's on-field struggles during his stay in New York.) Umpire Phil Lospitalier, normally a high school umpire, ruled a double play. That prompted Mets manager Joe Torre to emerge from the dugout. Torre contended that Clark had not made a clean transfer of the ball from glove to bare hand, thereby negating the catch according to the rules. The replacement umpires then held a conference and ruled in Torre's favor, allowing both Hebner to maintain his place on the base paths and permitting Mazzilli to reach base.

Not surprisingly, Giants manager Joe Altobelli reacted with some degree of rage to the reversal and promptly argued the umpires' decision. Apparently wanting to give both managers their due consideration, the umpiring crew met again—this time leaving the field completely, apparently so that they could confer in private. Upon their return, they produced a new call—the *third* call, for those keeping count.

Unlike the other two, this call was clearly a compromise aimed at satisfying both managers. The umpires ruled that Clark had made a legitimate catch on Mazzilli (producing one out), but deemed that Hebner could remain on base, since he had been confused by the indecisiveness of their original call. Much to the chagrin of the replacement umpires, neither Altobelli nor Torre were appeased. They both filed official protests with the National League office.

As it turned out, the call had little bearing on the game. The Mets won the game decidedly, by a count of 10-3, meaning that the umpires' decision had no direct effect on the outcome. All of the controversy overshadowed a milestone of sorts, as New York's Mike Scott picked up the first win of what would be a notable career.

The Third Call Counts—Part Two

The umpires just couldn't get the calls straight during Mets games in 1979.

In an August 21 game against the Houston Astros, the Mets needed three tries to record the 27th and final out at Shea Stadium. With two outs in the ninth inning and the Mets leading, 5-0, Houston's Jeff Leonard appeared to end the game with a routine fly ball out. The umpires said the pitch didn't count, however, since Mets shortstop Frank Taveras had called "timeout" only moments earlier. Given a reprieve, Leonard proceeded to line a single to left field. Well, that didn't *take* either. This time the umpires declared that Mets first baseman Ed Kranepool had not been given enough time to put himself into proper fielding position prior to the pitch to Leonard. The decision—an unusual one to say the least—prompted a protest from Astros manager Bill Virdon, but Leonard had to retrace his steps toward the plate and continue the never-ending at-bat. Leonard then flied out again, just as he had done the first time. This time, the play stood, the umpires offered no more reprieves, and the Mets had themselves a 5-0 win. And in a strange way, Leonard had gone 1-for-3 in one very unusual at-bat.

CHAPTER FIVE

The 1980s

Randy Jones

A t his best, Randy Jones threw a fastball that topped out in the low to mid-80s. Still, with one of the great change ups of his era, that was good enough to win the National League's Cy Young Award in 1976. Four winters later, the Mets hoped that a now fading Jones could recapture past glory; they acquired the soft-tossing left-hander from the San Diego Padres for pitcher John Pacella and infielder Jose Moreno. On the surface, the trade seemed like a good gamble for the Mets, but Jones continued to falter, in part because of his inability to pitch well at the ballpark in Queens.

As former Mets pitching coach Bill Monbouquette recalls, "I asked Randy Jones, 'Is there something wrong with Shea that you're struggling to pitch here?' You know, when I first came up in the big leagues, I was with San Diego, and Willie Mays hit a home run off me [at Shea]. I just haven't been the same since.' I said, 'Well, geez, Willie hit home runs off 600 other guys too, you know. So why *that?* I said to him, 'Hey, I'm an authority on home runs. I gave up 221 of them.' I said that just to ease his mind a little bit. But he struggled there."

Unfortunately, Jones continued to struggle with the Mets, at Shea, and in other places, eventually drawing his release. Even the best psychological efforts of "Monbo" couldn't help the onetime Cy Young Award winner.

King Kong

Just how bad were the Mets of the early 1980s? Even in leading the National League in an important statistical category, slugger Dave Kingman couldn't avoid a degree of ignominy. The free-swinging Kingman belted 37 home runs in 1982, good enough to lead all NL batters. Unfortunately, "King Kong" also batted a mere .204, giving him the unwanted title of worst batting average for a home run champion. It was no wonder the Mets traded him the first time around.

The Destroyer and Darling

The 1982 season marked two historic trades for the Mets. The first trade received far more publicity, but had little impact in improving the team's fortunes. The second trade, which paled in terms of newspaper ink, helped lay the foundation for the team's successes in the mid-1980s.

Just before the start of spring training, the Mets acquired one of the key components of the "Big Red Machine," one who was expected to provide them with a much-needed power hitter. In acquiring George "The Destroyer" Foster from the Reds, the Mets parted with only three players of middling value: catcher

Alex Trevino, flaky reliever Jim Kern (who was traded before he ever actually pitched for the Mets), and young right-hander Greg A. Harris. On the surface, it seemed like a steal for the Mets. Yet Foster struggled in making the adjustment from hitter-friendly Riverfront Stadium to pitcher-favorable Shea Stadium and failed to come close to matching the hallmark seasons he had experienced in Cincinnati.

By the end of his contract, which would pay him $2 million in 1986 (baseball's highest salary at the time), Foster had become arguably the most unpopular Met on the team. In the early stages of the 1986 seasons, fans at Shea Stadium booed him almost every time he came to the plate, and only relented after one New York City newspaper wrote about Foster's many contributions to charity. The reprieve didn't last. With the Mets on their way to winning the National League East in a runaway, the front office released the slumping Foster, who was hitting .227 at the time. Yet, Foster's lack of hitting had little to do with his sudden unemployment. The veteran left fielder had angered the Mets by hinting that the team was racist; he implied that management had demoted him from a starting role because he was black. Foster's allegation didn't seem to have much basis in logic, given that one of his immediate replacements in left field was Kevin Mitchell, also an African American. Foster then damaged his public image and his credibility even further by failing to show up for a scheduled appearance on Art Rust Jr.'s popular nighttime sports talk show. Rust, also an African American, roundly criticized Foster for his unwillingness to fulfill the media appointment.

While the Foster deal ended in disappointment, another 1982 trade resulted in long-term dividends. On April 1, the Mets incurred the wrath of their fans by trading popular outfielder (and teen idol and overall sex symbol) Lee Mazzilli to the Texas Rangers for two unknown pitchers. The two young right-handers—Ron Darling and Walt Terrell—would become dependable parts of the Mets' five-man rotation. Darling would remain in New York through the team's glory years, making three starts in the 1986 World Series, while Terrell was later traded for slugging infielder Howard Johnson.

From Teen Idol to Journeyman

Lee Mazzilli's fade from All-Star player to journeyman before the age of 30 remains one of the great Met mysteries. As Steve Treder of *The Hardball Times* recalls, Mazzilli suffered an inexplicable decline. "Always a popular figure in New York," says Treder, "Mazzilli from 1978 to 1980 was one of the better young players in baseball, the complete package of power, speed, and on-base ability. But at age 26 in 1981, he slumped badly. The Mets traded him away [in the deal that shrewdly netted Ron Darling], and he was never more than a utility player for the rest of his career."

Mazzilli did earn a brief encore for the Mets, however. Though no longer an everyday player, Maz returned to the Mets as a key pinch-hitter late in the 1986 championship season.

Seeing Isn't Necessarily Believing

During his early 1980s stint as the Mets' pitching coach, Bill Monbouquette was given the task of working with a group of very talented, but also very raw, group of pitchers. One particularly tall and talented right-handed starter presented Monbouquette with his largest challenge.

"Mike Scott was a guy that was kind of set in his own ways. One day [manager] George Bamberger says, 'Let's show him the film [of himself pitching].' So we're going over the film and I'm saying, 'See this and that.' And he said, 'That's not me [on the film].' I said, 'Scotty, Mike, that's you.' And he says [again], 'No, that's not me.' So I walked back into George Bamberger's office. He says, 'I thought you were showing him [the film].' I said, 'George, you're not going to believe this, but he thinks it's not him on the film.' And George is going, 'What?!' I said, 'George, don't worry about it; I will take care of it.' So Bamberger asked me, 'What are you gonna do now?'"

As it turns out, Monbouquette had a backup plan.

"When Scott was pitching at Tidewater, I was in charge of minor league pitchers. It was a day off and they had a big cookout, and I got invited. I got to talking to his wife about how tough it was to work with Mike, since he was so set in his ways. She said, 'If you have a problem, you just come get me.' So I remembered that."

The lesson for pitching coaches? If you're having problems with one of your pitchers, just talk to his better half.

Bambi and the Swan

Bill Monbouquette recalls an incident involving a struggling pitcher, a member of the team's front office, manager George Bamberger, and several coaches.

"I can remember one time coming back from St. Louis. We had played terrible on the road. We were delayed in St. Louis [at the airport]. So we all went into the bar and we're having a couple of beers. And then they come back and say OK, the plane's getting set. We got on the plane and arrived at LaGuardia. And we got on the bus, and Craig Swan, who had a couple of beers too many—he said something nasty to Arthur Richman. Swannie was a character. He was struggling, he was having tough times. [Manager] George [Bamberger] was deaf, I think in this [the right] ear, and he didn't hear [Swan's remark]. And so George said he didn't hear it. So I told him, 'You better get him and go over and talk to him.' So we got to Shea. George got off the bus; he sat in the front. We were waiting for Swan. And everybody was off the bus. And here comes Swannie, and I was heading right for his car [which was located near the bus]. Because I had told him, 'George wants to talk to you.' So he was stooped over his car. And I went over there, right by the bus, and I said, 'Hey, you're not going nowhere.' He tried to get away. So I grabbed him. He was a big guy, and we we are struggling."

Within moments, Monbouquette received some help from the team's largest coach, who outweighed Swan by 50 to 60 pounds.

"All of a sudden, boom, here comes Frank Howard," says a relieved Monbouquette. "Frank grabbed him—and Swannie couldn't get away. And the bus was going back and forth, like this. And Bobby Bailor, who was the last one getting off the bus—as he was getting off, he said, 'Gee, the bus is rocking!' And I was holding on! So we got him into George's room in the clubhouse. We talked to him about some things, and he apologized."

Thankfully, Howard's presence helped diffuse the situation, with his six-foot-seven, 280-pound frame forming a needed combination of intimidation and deterrence.

"Frank was a nice, easy-going guy," says Monbouquette. "But, I'll tell you what, I'd hate for him to be mad at me [given his size and strength]. Thank God he was the 'Gentle Giant.'"

Otherwise, Swan might have landed on the disabled list in addition to landing in Bamberger's doghouse.

In Search of a Reliever

Prior to the development of Jesse Orosco, who shared the closer duties for the 1986 world champions, the Mets relied on curveballing Neil Allen as their bullpen ace. Pitching coach Bill Monbouquette remembers well the exploits of Allen, a flaky right-hander with a high-pitched voice who later became the bullpen coach for the cross-town Yankees. "Neil Allen, of course, was a character. One time, George Bamberger said to me to stay down in the bullpen for a couple of days. And the phone rang. I said, 'Allen, get up.'"

Allen, however, made no effort to move from his position in the bullpen.

"I looked around and said, 'Are you gonna get up?' Allen said, 'I can't find my glove.' And I happened to look down; he didn't even have spikes on. I said, 'You know something, you're starting to aggravate me!'"

On another occasion, with Monbouquette in his more accustomed position in the dugout, Allen caused additional consternation for the pitching coach.

"I can remember one day when George Bamberger said to get Allen [warmed] up. So I called down to the bullpen. Then I was looking from the bench and I didn't see anyone going. I told George, 'He's not up.' So I called down there again. Bamberger said, 'Go down there.' I had to go up, then go all the way underneath the tunnel, and all the way over to the bullpen. As I got there, I saw hamburger wrappers, pizza boxes. One time I found a guy, he was delivering pizzas back of the garden there. He was slipping the pizzas under the fence. So when I got down there, I said, 'Well, where's Allen?' They told me he had to go down to the bathroom in the clubhouse. So I went down to the clubhouse and I was looking for him, I couldn't find him. I walked into the manager's room; there he was, his feet up on the desk, watching the television, eating a hamburger. I said to him, 'Do you know that you're supposed to be up and throwing right now?' He said, 'No.' I said, 'Of course, you don't.' So he said, 'OK!' in that high squeaky voice of his, and away he went!"

Tom Terrific: Part Two

In a classic case of trying rectify a past mistake, the Mets used part of the 1982 off season to reacquire franchise pitcher Tom Seaver. In trading pitcher Charlie Puleo and minor leaguers Lloyd McClendon (a catcher) and Jason Felice (an outfielder) to the Reds, the Mets tried to reverse the fateful 1977 "Midnight Massacre" trade that had sent him away.

In bringing back "Tom Terrific," the Mets hoped to improve their 1983 pitching staff while also making public relations points with their diminishing fan base. Seaver's impact on the team's fans would be felt right away, beginning with Opening Day at Shea Stadium. Tabbed to start the opener by manager George Bamberger, Seaver would find his normal pre-game routine altered as part of an effort to satisfy the Shea Stadium faithful.

"I was a real creature of habit: sleep, diet, exercise," says Seaver. "Not being superstitious, but if you wanted to be consistent, you did the same things all the time. [As usual] I warmed up in the bullpen on Opening Day. Then Jay Horwitz [the Mets' head of public relations] came up to me and asked me to walk down the right-field line to the dugout. I was going to do it the way I always did it, walk under the tunnel, go through the clubhouse, put on a dry shirt, go back out and pitch. Jay came to me and said, 'Will you walk down the right-field line instead?'"

Horwitz wanted Seaver to walk along that more public path so that the fans would have a chance to give him a standing ovation.

"Jay and I, we were very good friends," Seaver says. "And he would not have asked me to do it unless it meant something to him. Well, I didn't want to do it [disrupt my routine] because I was worried about the game."

Still, Seaver relented.

"And then I started walking down the right-field line and I realized what Jay was talking about. The emotional reaction of the crowd … I have some pictures of that day. It was a terrific memory."

Seaver's Second Departure

Tom Seaver would pitch reasonably well in 1983, posting a record of 9-14 with a respectable 3.55 ERA, but he didn't come close to achieving the level of stardom the Mets had witnessed during his first stint in New York. Sadly, the last of those prime years had come and gone—during his in-between tenure with the Reds. In baseball, seven years is an awfully long time. In the case of Tom Seaver, it marked the difference between being a dominant superstar pitcher and being a run-of-the-mill No. 3 starter.

Seaver's second tenure in New York lasted only one season. As part of the new and complicated compensation system attached to baseball free agency, the Mets lost Seaver to the Chicago White Sox in a special wintertime draft. The Mets hadn't even signed White Sox free agent Dennis Lamp (who actually signed with the Toronto Blue Jays); under the new system, a team losing a free agent could select any player left unprotected by any major league team. The Mets, who had left Seaver off their protected list prior to the compensation draft, thus lost

"The Franchise" for a second time. As a result, Mets fans would be deprived of watching Seaver win his 300th game while wearing the blue and orange of the Mets. Instead, he won the milestone game wearing the pajama-like togs of the Chicago White Sox, claiming No. 300 at Yankee Stadium, no less.

You Can't Sign Them All

Headlined by the selections of such players as Dwight Gooden and Darryl Strawberry, the Mets' drafts of the 1980s provided an excess of talent for the organization. While some detractors might point out that the Mets couldn't help but draft talented players because of their favorable drafting position, the organization deserves credit for doing a good job of signing the young players—and generally to reasonable contracts. Yet, there was at least one future star who did get away.

In June of 1983, the Mets drafted a young infielder named Matt Williams out of high school, but were unable to sign him to a professional contract. Three years later, the San Francisco Giants took the same Matt Williams, who would become a perennial All-Star third baseman in the Bay Area and eventually contribute to a world championship with the Arizona Diamondbacks in 2001.

Same Names

I love names. Odd names, made-up names, tough-to-pronounce names. I also like shared names, in other words, when a less famous person happens to have the same name as a superstar or legendary figure. Over the years, the Mets have had a few players who shared names with more famous players, or in some cases, cultural icons and even restaurants. Here are a few, with their years as Mets indicated in parentheses:

Bob Gibson (1987): Like the St. Louis Cardinals' Hall of Fame ace of the 1960s, this Bob Gibson threw with his right arm and threw very hard. End of similarities. This obscure journeyman lacked control and an effective breaking pitch in toiling for the Milwaukee Brewers and the Mets, with whom he made one brief appearance at the tail end of his career in 1987. At his peak, he did save 11 games and helped set up Hall of Famer Rollie Fingers in Milwaukee's bullpen during the 1985 season.

Brian Giles (1981-83): This former Met second baseman hit so ineffectively and gained such a poor reputation for lackadaisical play that teammate John Stearns once called him a "jive turkey." The current-day Brian Giles, one of the better hitters among National League outfielders, plays the game much harder and has been one of the lesser-publicized stars in either league. The younger Giles also looks an awful lot like Lenny Dykstra, at least after "Nails" started hitting the weights.

Howard Johnson (1985-93): The former Mets star, best known for his 30-30 capabilities, is perhaps the only player in major league history to share his name with a hotel chain—and a restaurant. In the late 1970s and early 1980s, the Mets also featured a career minor league player whose name coincided with that of a restaurant "character." The player? Infielder Ronald MacDonald. We kid you not.

The Best First Baseman in Franchise History

If the acquisition of Ron Darling was the first key trade in assembling the eventual world championship team of 1986, then the deal that brought Keith Hernandez to New York was the first *blockbuster* trade that laid the groundwork for future greatness. On June 15, 1983, the Mets put the finishing touches on a pivotal three-player deal with the St. Louis Cardinals. Surrendering reliever Neil Allen and pitching prospect Rick Ownbey, the Mets acquired Hernandez, who had won the batting title with a .344 mark and shared National League MVP honors only four years earlier but had also experienced drug problems while with the Cardinals. Overly anxious to rid the team of Hernandez, Cardinals general manager (and manager) Whitey Herzog sold off his talented first baseman at a bargain basement price. The Mets benefited from Herzog's ill-timed trade, giving up two expendable pitchers for an All-Star first baseman, Gold Glove fielder, and legitimate No. 3 hitter.

By now recovered from his drug problems, Hernandez would become the best first baseman in Mets history while also bringing needed doses of intelligence and leadership to a young clubhouse filled with players who didn't yet know how to win. That atmosphere would continue to change, especially with the coming arrival of another All-Star, Gary Carter.

The Kid Comes to Queens

Just call it "The Trade." No transaction was more important to the well being of the Mets franchise than the trade that general manager Frank Cashen made on December 10, 1984. That's the day that Cashen sent a package of four players, headed up by the talented and versatile Hubie Brooks, to the Montreal Expos for the National League's best catcher in Gary "The Kid" Carter. While Brooks was a fine player for New York and would go on to become a mainstay in Montreal, he was no match for Carter. And the three other players in the deal—catcher Mike Fitzgerald, outfielder Herm Winningham, and minor league pitcher Floyd Youmans—didn't come close to making the trade an even one for the Expos. After all, Carter was a Hall of Fame talent with boisterous leadership skills and a zealous desire to win. Simply put, he was a perfect fit for a team searching for a catcher and looking for a veteran hand to guide an assemblage of talented but young players.

Given his reputation as an All-Star catcher, Mets fans expected Carter to raise the team's level of play. He did that immediately, slamming a game-ending home run against former Mets reliever Neil Allen on Opening Day in 1985.

"That was a special moment because earlier in the game I got hit in the elbow by Joaquin Andujar," Carter says. "And it was a cold, blustery, windy day. If it hadn't been Opening Day, and because there was so much emphasis placed on what Gary Carter was going to mean to the Mets … I might have come out of the game [under other circumstances]. I remember putting some ice on the elbow during the course of the game, but it was so cold you really didn't need ice. Nevertheless, I was putting it on the elbow to relieve the discomfort."

The pain started to dissipate when Carter achieved his first milestone as a Met.

"Finally, I got a hit in the middle innings. When I got that hit—it was a double in the gap—the fans applauded and cheered and really made me feel welcome. When that happened, I kind of felt this relief. As the game progressed and we went into extra

Gary Carter—The best all-round catcher in the history of the franchise became the first member of the 1986 Mets to make the Hall of Fame.
PHOTO FILE/Landov

innings, I came up in that situation against Allen. Neil threw me a first-pitch curveball—he was always known for his big curveball—and he missed with it. I said to myself, 'You know what, I'm going to sit on another breaking ball.' He kind of left it out over the plate."

Carter extended his arms and pulled the pitch to left field. The ball barely cleared the left-field wall, giving the Mets a dramatic win on Opening Day and making Carter an instant sensation at Shea Stadium.

"As I left the field and was walking into the dugout," Carter recalls, "the fans started chanting my name. That endeared me and made me feel so welcome to the city of New York [in a way] that I had never felt before during the 10 previous years in Montreal."

Motivated by the fans at Shea, Carter decided to step out of the dugout and tip his cap.

"There was a trend, of curtain calls, that maybe started with that Opening Day," says Carter. "I was just so elated and happy that I made that contribution. We won the first game I was in a Met uniform, and I was just so excited about that."

The Curious Case of Sidd Finch

There has been no greater hoax in the history of the Mets than the case of Sidd Finch—and the Mets had nothing to do with it. It was completely the product of the creative genius of legendary sportswriter George Plimpton.

During the spring of 1985, the famed writer penned a fictitious article for *Sports Illustrated* about a top-notch Mets pitching prospect with the curious name of Sidd Finch, whom Plimpton described as having a 168-mph fastball. Plimpton wrote the April Fool's Day article in such a believable style that more than a few readers, including some diehard Mets fans, regarded Finch as a real prospect, only to learn later that Plimpton had perpetrated one of the greatest fabrications in baseball's literary history.

The Rick Camp Game

As baseball fans, most of the games we tend to remember occurred during the postseason, especially the Championship Series and the World Series. Sometimes regular season games, because of the sheer volume of them, become lost in our collective memories. Yet almost any Mets fan born in the 1970s or earlier has some recollection of the game the Mets played against the Atlanta Braves on July 4, 1985—and didn't finish until well into July 5.

In what some have come to call "The Rick Camp Game," the Mets and Braves played 19 innings over the course of those two dates. Keith Hernandez, enjoying one of his finest nights as a Met, hit for the cycle. On two occasions, the Mets had to sit out rain delays on a humid night in Atlanta. And then there were the events of the last two innings, including one of the unlikeliest home runs in professional baseball history.

In the top of the 18th, the Mets scored to take an 11-10 lead. After Mets pitcher Tom Gorman retired the first two Braves batters in the bottom half of the inning, a win seemed like an inevitable lock for the Mets. That's because the next scheduled batter for the Braves was light-hitting pitcher Rick Camp. Just how light hitting? For some old-time baseball fans, Camp, an .062 lifetime batter, stirred up bad memories of Ron Herbel, a onetime pitcher with the Mets who accumulated the worst batting average of any major league player with at least 200 at-bats. (Just how much of a struggle was it for Herbel with a bat in his hands? In 206 major league at-bats, Herbel accumulated a total

Arguably the greatest defensive first baseman in modern day history, Keith Hernandez displays his usual form of balance and grace.
Stephen Dunn/Getty Images

of six hits. That's *six*, not *sixteen*. Six hits in 206 at-bats, for an average of .029—and no home runs.)

With no players left on their bench, the Braves had no choice but to let Camp hit for himself. Fully expected to strike out to end the game, Camp decided that more baseball needed to be played. He promptly blasted a solo home run, tying the game at 11-11.

At that point, the Mets might have been expected to fold up their uniforms, head home, and make way for the Fourth of July postgame fireworks display the Braves had planned. Instead, the Mets rallied for five runs in the top of the 19th, with three runs coming home on a Danny Heep single, to take a 16-11 lead.

Refusing to give up, the Braves rallied for two runs against starter-turned-reliever Ron Darling in the bottom half of the 19th. They were helped by—of all things—an error by the usually flawless Keith Hernandez. Then, in a case of déjà vu, Camp came to the plate during the inning, again with two outs. This time Camp did what he did routinely with a bat in hand—he struck out, ending the game at 3:55 in the morning.

Six minutes later, at just after four o'clock in the morning, the fireworks show began. A few of the 44,947 fans at Fulton County Stadium even stayed around to watch it.

Wally Backman

Pound for pound, Wally Backman may have been the toughest player the Mets have ever had. The five-foot-nine, 160-pound second baseman once challenged the largest man on the team, six-foot-six Darryl Strawberry, to a wrestling match—and won. Brash and outspoken beyond usual limits, Backman once publicly blasted star teammate George Foster for failing to join the rest of the Mets in a bench-clearing brawl. As Foster remained in the dugout, Backman seethed at what he considered an act of disloyalty to the team. Unlike many players of lesser talents who publicly berate better-known teammates, Backman outlasted Foster in wearing a Mets uniform. Backman remained with the

Mets through 1988 while Foster drew his release in the midst of the 1986 world championship season.

Unfortunately, the fire-and-brimstone approach that made Backman an overachiever on the field may have contributed to eventual problems away from the diamond. After his playing days, Backman was arrested on separate charges of fighting with his wife and driving under the influence. When those arrests became publicly known, Backman was fired as manager of the Arizona Diamondbacks—only four days after winning the job.

CHAPTER SIX

1986 and Beyond

The Trade That Never Was

Ray Knight is best remembered as the emotional leader and World Series MVP of the 1986 Mets, but the veteran third baseman almost didn't make it through spring training with the club. Due to his injury-plagued 1985 season, some members of the Mets' front office had soured on Knight. With the talented Howard Johnson waiting to take over third base, Knight seemed expendable. Knight's lack of versatility also posed a problem; if he were to be benched in favor of "HoJo," he could play only one other position—first base—which was already occupied by All-Star Keith Hernandez. As a result, Knight didn't figure to receive much playing time as a backup.

As a result, the Mets considered releasing Knight during spring training in 1986. Not wanting to lose him outright, the Mets shopped Knight to other teams throughout the spring. According to one report, the Mets engaged in some serious trade discussions with the Chicago Cubs. Although other players were

Though a journeyman for most of his career, Ray Knight reached the heights of stardom throughout the regular season and postseason of 1986. Rich Pilling/MLB Photos/Getty Images

rumored to be included, the centerpiece of the trade would involve Knight going to the Cubs for veteran infielder-outfielder Davey Lopes. The trade seemed make some sense for the Mets; Lopes would give the Mets more speed, along with the versatility to play second base, third base, and any of the outfield positions.

At one point, the Mets thought they had completed the trade with the Cubs. Moments later, the deal fell apart—thankfully for the Mets. If it hadn't, the Mets might not have won the National League Championship Series (NLCS) against the Houston Astros or the World Series against the Boston Red Sox.

There is one footnote to the story. The Cubs did wind up trading Davey Lopes to a contender: the Houston Astros. He appeared in three games against the Mets in the aforementioned NLCS.

HoJo's Ribs

Due to Ray Knight's resurgence in 1986, Howard Johnson appeared in only 88 regular season games and generally played a background role for the world champions. In some ways, the individual highlight of Johnson's year took place before the season—in the annual rib-eating contest held at Rusty Staub's popular New York City restaurant. With dozens of New York area athletes participating, a ravenous Johnson tied for first place in the gluttonous competition. Johnson ate 36 ribs in only three minutes (an amazing 12 per minute). Even more impressively, Johnson's culinary habits matched those of a football player, as he shared the crown with fullback Rocky Klever of the NFL's New York Jets.

Ribs aside, HoJo would account for one of the biggest hits of the regular season, at least from an emotional standpoint. On

April 24, his dramatic two-run homer against Todd Worrell in the ninth inning tied a key divisional game against the Cardinals. The Mets won the game in the next inning and were never threatened again by the defending National League champions.

Mookie and Lenny

Everything went right for the Mets in 1986. Even injuries produced unexpected benefits. On March 5, starting center fielder Mookie Wilson suffered a badly damaged eye while participating in a spring training base running drill. A ball thrown by shortstop Rafael Santana struck Wilson in the right eye, shattering the protective safety glasses he was wearing. The incident left Wilson with splinters from the protective glass *in* his eye and resulted in 17 stitches just *above* the eye. The Mets expected Wilson to miss six weeks, meaning that he would have to start the regular season on the 15-day disabled list.

With Wilson sidelined, manager Davey Johnson turned to his young backup center fielder, Lenny Dykstra. The youngster's cockiness turned off some opponents, but merely reflected a strong confidence in his own abilities. Dykstra had reason to be cocky; he became a dynamic leadoff hitter (far better suited for the role than the free-swinging Wilson) and flashed an abundance of speed and range in the outfield. By the All-Star break, Dykstra's batting average resided at a robust .349. Even after Wilson's return from the disabled list, Dykstra remained in center field—where he belonged.

"Marry Me, Lenny"

Lenny Dykstra's hitting captured the attention of manager Davey Johnson and the rest of the Mets brass, but it was his boyish good looks that opened the eyes of some of his most ardent fans. One fan in particular became particularly enamored of Dykstra during the 1986 season. A young woman, wearing a bridal dress and carrying a sign that said "Marry Me, Lenny," attended a number of games at Shea Stadium. The wedding wannabe even took the unusual show on the road, attending a game at Wrigley Field on August 4 with full bridal regalia and her sign of proposal still in hand. The obsessive fan faced at least one obstacle, however, of which she may not have been aware. Dykstra, though young and handsome and an obvious catch, was already married.

Playing Without a Full Deck

It's not very well remembered, but the Mets actually won the world championship in 1986 with only a 24-man roster—and not the usual 25-man team. Then again, all of the other teams employed 24 men on each of their rosters, too. Via a gentleman's agreement, each of the 26 major league teams had decided to forego using a 25th player, as a way of saving some money in salary and travel expenses. Although the Mets willingly played along with the decision, manager Davey Johnson abhorred the lack of an extra player. As a manager who platooned his players at several positions and liked to make frequent substitutions during games, Johnson felt the new roster limited his ability to maneuver.

The absence of a 25th man irritated Johnson from the start of the season. In the Mets' home opener, Johnson used pitcher

**Intelligent, innovative, and combative, Davey Johnson skillfully
shuffled the Mets' 24-man roster in 1986.** Mike Powell/Getty Images

Rick Aguilera as a pinch-hitter since he used all of his position
players. In the same game, Johnson had to utilize second baseman Tim Teufel at first base, a position he had never before
played in the major leagues.

In spite of Johnson's objections, the Mets raced out to a 20-
5 start in 1986. Johnson still did his best to shuffle his lineups
accordingly, using at least two players at each position through
the first 25 games of the season. So for those who think that
Johnson merely sat back and watched a talented team run away
with the National League East, think again. The man did more

mixing and matching than the average major league manager, while trying to overcome a roster limit that he simply despised.

A Different Kind of Shortstop

Prior to the modern era that featured heavy-hitting short-stops like Nomar Garciaparra, Derek Jeter, and Miguel Tejada, most major league teams emphasized defensive play over offense prowess in filling the key middle infield position. For years major league managers talked breathlessly about the importance of having a good defensive shortstop, even if it meant carrying a light hitter at the backend of the batting order.

In 1986, Davey Johnson proved to be a progressive thinker by contradicting that traditional managerial preference. He often benched the sure handed Rafael Santana in favor of converted third basemen—and harder hitters—like Howard Johnson and rookie Kevin Mitchell.

"When I fill out the lineup card every game, my first priority is putting the best offensive club out there possible against the opposing pitcher," Johnson explained to Bill Conlin of *The Sporting News*. "I figure if we score enough runs, the defense will take care of itself."

The use of Mitchell at shortstop was especially intriguing. Regarded as a third baseman-outfielder at the beginning of spring training, Mitchell had virtually no experience as a shortstop. Then, in the final exhibition game of the spring, Johnson started Mitchell at short and watched him handle nine chances without an error. That performance convinced Johnson that the talented rookie could handle the position on a part-time basis.

With Mitchell providing an unexpected power boost to the lineup, Johnson continued to rotate his three shortstops over the first half of the season. After the All-Star break, with the Mets having built up a hefty lead in the National League East, Johnson turned conservative; becoming concerned about Mitchell and Johnson's frequent errors, he decided to back off his unusual three-man platoon and reinstate Santana as the No. 1 shortstop. Still, while it lasted, the use of a big hitter at shortstop made the 1986 Mets look more like a power-laden team of the 2000s.

The Race Card

In late July, Davey Johnson made another intriguing lineup change. Having grown tired of George Foster's frequent strike-outs, Johnson benched "The Destroyer," replacing him with a platoon of Kevin Mitchell and Danny Heep. When asked about the demotion, Foster offered a response that would quickly anger Johnson and the rest of Mets management.

"I'm not saying it's a racial thing," Foster reportedly told a Chicago sportswriter, "but that seems to be the case in sports these days. When a ball club can, they replace a George Foster or a Mookie Wilson with a more popular player."

In other words, the Mets were seizing opportunities to replace black players with white ones.

Foster later denied making the controversial comments, and then denied that he had called the Mets racist. Neither Davey Johnson nor key members of the Mets front office believed Foster's denials. The alleged comments particularly infuriated Johnson, who didn't like the implication that he made lineup decisions based on race, and also felt that he had been patient and fair with Foster, giving him every chance to regain his hitting stroke. Johnson confronted Foster about the remarks, but the outfielder walked away. Johnson recommended that the front office release Foster, which general manager Frank Cashen did officially on August 7.

If Foster did indeed make the comments suggesting racism on the part of the Mets, they didn't make complete sense. Wilson had been injured in the spring, allowing Dykstra to move into the starting lineup. If Johnson had returned the hot-hitting Dykstra to the bench after Wilson's returned, he would have been skewered by the New York media—and rightfully so. As for Foster's situation, he had been replaced initially by a platoon of one black player (Mitchell) and one white player (Heep). Later on, Johnson would replace Heep with Wilson, making the left-field arrangement a platoon of two black players. While the Mets had been rightfully accused of being racist in past years, allegations of racial prejudice just didn't fit the bill in 1986.

Sons of the Father

While the roster of the 1986 Mets read like a "Who's Who" of baseball, the organization's minor league system also featured its share of intriguing names. With the signing of amateurs Bill Robinson III and Jamie Roseboro, the Mets' farm clubs included four sons of former major leaguers. Robinson III, an outfielder and the son of former major league outfielder and then Mets coach Bill Robinson, played for Little Falls of the NY-Penn League, as did catcher Jamie Roseboro, the son of former Los Angeles Dodgers receiver John Roseboro. Robinson III and the younger Roseboro joined two holdovers from the Mets' farm system. Infielder Craig Repoz, the son of former Yankees outfielder Roger Repoz, starred for Columbia of the South Atlantic League. One of his teammates with Columbia was outfielder Scott Jaster, the son of former St. Louis Cardinals left-hander Larry Jaster.

All four of the second-generation youngsters put up good numbers for their minor league teams in 1986. Yet, none of the

four ever matched their fathers in making the always difficult
jump to the big leagues.

Knight vs. Davis

Davey Johnson called it the "strangest game I've ever been
involved in."

On July 22, the Reds hosted the Mets in what would
become a hallmark game for the New York franchise. Three different incidents resulted in five players and one coach being ejected from the game. The nastiest melee took place in the bottom
of the 10th inning, when Eric Davis stole third base. As Davis
slid into third, he bumped Ray Knight, who was covering the
bag. The two players then exchanged shoves. Not satisfied with
that show of anger, Knight hurled a punch at Davis that landed
squarely.

"He elbowed me at the end of the play," Knight explained,
"and I said to him, 'What's your problem?'" According to Knight,
Davis responded by saying, "*You* pushed me."

Both Knight and Davis earned ejections for their share in
the histrionics, as did the Mets' Kevin Mitchell and Cincinnati's
Mario Soto. (Darryl Strawberry had previously been ejected in
the sixth inning for arguing balls and strikes.) The brawl that
resulted from the Davis-Knight showdown represented the
fourth—and most severe—on-field fight for the Mets that season. The game featured another incident of notoriety. During
that same 10th inning, Davey Johnson alternated Jesse Orosco
and Roger McDowell between pitching and playing right field,
so that he could match each hurler up against a Reds batter without removing him from the game. Orosco and McDowell repeated the position switch in the 11th and 13th innings. And in the
12th, McDowell rotated between left and right field. Thankfully

for Johnson and the Mets, none of the Reds' batters hit a ball toward the pitchers-turned-outfielders until the 13th, when Tony Perez lofted a fly ball to Orosco in right. Orosco made the catch, sparing Johnson the nightmare of watching a pitcher aimlessly swat his glove in the direction of a fly ball.

The Mets finally won the game in the 14th inning, when Howard Johnson clubbed a three-run homer. McDowell, who was on the mound at the right time, earned the win.

Darling vs. Davey

Few pitchers combined the smarts, talents, and looks of Ron Darling. A graduate of Yale University, Darling developed as a top prospect with the Texas Rangers organization before being sent to the Mets in a three-player trade. By 1986, Darling had firmly established himself as a durable fixture in the Mets' heralded starting rotation—and as a cover boy for an in-season issue of *Gentleman's Quarterly* magazine. Yet, Darling lacked the approval of Davey Johnson, who felt that the articulate right-hander tended to nibble against opposing hitters, thereby walking too many batters and running up high pitch counts. Darling, recognizing the distance between himself and Johnson, blamed the manager—a former major league second baseman—for their stalled relationship.

"Davey Johnson hasn't spoken to me three times all season," Darling told *Gentleman's Quarterly*. "He doesn't believe in communicating with his players. Some players maybe—Ray Knight or Keith Hernandez—but not pitchers. Pitchers are not *players*, you understand, and Davey Johnson was a player."

Fighting Words

The 1986 National League Championship Series between the Mets and the Houston Astros may have been the most thrilling series since the adoption of the playoffs in 1969. It also produced a memorable exchange on the mound, occurring in the latter moments of the climactic sixth game at the Houston Astrodome.

Playing in the top of the 16th inning, the Mets scored three times to take a 6-3 lead over Houston. The Astros, who had rallied to tie the game against Jesse Orosco in the 14th, put pressure on the lefty again, scoring two runs and placing two more runners on base with two men out. With the switch-hitting Kevin Bass coming to the plate in a position to tie or win the game, Gary Carter and Keith Hernandez met with Orosco on the mound. Hernandez, seizing control of the conversation, made it clear that he did not like Carter's pitch selection during the inning. "Kid," said Hernandez, addressing Carter by his nickname, "if you call one more fastball, we're going to fight."

Carter listened to Hernandez' advice—or warning. The veteran catcher called for six consecutive sliders. With the count three-and-two, Orosco struck out Bass—with slider No. 6. With that pitch, the Mets won the game and the Series, and Carter avoided having to brawl with one of his own teammates.

The Buckner Game

Game 6 of the 1986 World Series ranks among the top five games in Fall Classic history. With the Red Sox leading by two runs, no one on base, and two men out in the bottom of the 10th, the Mets found themselves on the verge of elimination. Given their regular season excesses, a World Series loss (in six games, no less) would have been regarded as sheer failure by the majority of New York City's media and fan base.

That possibility didn't seem to bother Gary Carter as he stepped into the batter's box at Shea Stadium.

"The feeling that I had when I came to the plate was one of confidence. I've always felt that way because I like those kinds of pressure situations," Carter says. "And I didn't really want to be the answer to the trivia question: 'Who was going to make the last out of the World Series in 1986?' I'm standing up there after Wally Backman and Keith Hernandez had made outs, and everybody I think in the stadium thought it was over. The Boston Red Sox were starting to celebrate—I was told that Dennis 'Oil Can' Boyd had already gone into the clubhouse and had already opened up a champagne bottle.

"But I like the old theory that Yogi Berra made famous. 'It's not over till it's over.' That's the way we played all year. That was the character of our ball club. We were a late-inning, rallying type of team. I was gonna do whatever I could to reach first base, scratch, claw, whatever it was gonna take to get on first base. … I just felt that I was going to come through."

Carter did, lifting a single into left field. Kevin Mitchell and Ray Knight followed Carter's lead with two more singles, bringing the Mets within a run and putting the tying run on third base. With Mookie Wilson at the plate, Bob Stanley threw a pitch down and in that eluded catcher Rich Gedman, allowing the tying run to score and the potential winning run to move into scoring position. (Though Stanley was charged with a wild pitch, Gedman should have been held accountable with a passed ball.) Wilson then chopped a bouncer down the first base line. Playing on bad knees, an aging Bill Buckner backtracked, then let the ball slide in between his legs and down the right-field line. It's debatable whether Buckner would have had a play on the speedy

Wilson at first, but the error permitted the game-winning run to score. After the game, Red Sox manager John McNamara faced a barrage of questioning surrounding his decision not to use utility man Dave Stapleton as a defensive caddy for a hobbled Buckner, a maneuver that he had used through the regular season.

After watching the ball trickle through Buckner's legs, Carter felt confident about the eventual outcome of the Series.

"To us, we felt, 'Now we have the momentum.' And it didn't matter what was going to happen in Game 7, we were gonna win."

The Mets would fall behind, 3-0, in the seventh game, but the team retained its swagger and stormed back to win, 8-5, to claim the second world championship in franchise history. It was something that would not have happened if Carter hadn't delivered that two-out single with the season on the brink.

A Share for Public Relations

Suffice to say, the Mets were not a well-liked team in 1986. Opponents considered Mets players cocky to the point of arrogance. National League teams grew angry with New York's repeated "curtain calls" after home runs, even after meaningless long balls in one-sided games. The dislike for the Mets became even more intense as the team piled up lopsided wins, embarrassing the rest of the league in running away with the Eastern Division title.

Yet, after the World Series, the Mets did something that belied their hated reputation as gloating winners. The players on the Mets voted a three-quarters share of postseason money to the team's public relations director, Jay Horwitz. It was believed to be the first time that a World Series winner had ever given even a partial share of postseason money to the team's publicity man.

The Mets deserved credit for recognizing the time-consuming role that Horwitz had played in fulfilling his duties as the head of the team's public relations efforts. During the postseason, Horwitz repeatedly worked into the wee hours of the morning arranging interviews and handling other media requests. On one occasion, Horwitz stayed late to help one of the members of the media find a hotel room. Horwitz found the stranded sportswriter a room—at four o'clock in the morning.

A Backup Catcher for an Ace

At the time, it hardly created a stir. Within two seasons, it would start to produce a boatload of high-dividend returns. During the spring of 1987, the defending world champion Mets traded backup catcher Ed Hearn and two throw-in pitchers to the Kansas City Royals for minor leaguer Chris Jelic and a young pitcher named David Cone.

Only baseball diehards knew about Cone's value as a prospect. To most fans and followers of the game, Cone was simply a no-name. How unknown was Cone? A sporting goods company that supplied major leaguers with equipment sent Cone a special bat personally engraved with his name on it. The name on the bat read "David Cohen."

Sporting goods companies and fans of the game wouldn't mistake Cone's identity for long. Over the next five and a half seasons with the Mets, Cone would win 80 games, highlighted by a 20-3 season in 1988. Throwing an assortment of pitches from a variety of arm angles, the creative right-hander would lead the league in strikeouts in both 1990 and 1991. He would continue his dominance even after his departure from the Mets, winning the American League's Cy Young Award in 1994 and hurling a perfect game in 1999. It's safe to say that few people, if any, have ever made the mistake of calling him "Mr. Cohen" again.

Doc's Downfall

With a formidable starting rotation of Doc Gooden, Sid Fernandez, Ron Darling, and Bobby Ojeda returning from the world championship roster, there didn't appear to be a crying need for another starting pitcher in 1987. Yet, Mets management realized that pitching depth could become eradicated quicker than any other part of a roster, given the fragility of pitchers' arms. And then there was a problem with drugs—one that may not have been foreseen the day the Mets made the deal for David Cone. Gooden, who would test positive for cocaine use later in the spring, would begin a scheduled month-long rehabilitation stay at the Smithers Clinic on April 2, less than a week before Opening Day. With the loss of Gooden, their full-fledged staff ace, the Mets' starting rotation suddenly didn't seem nearly as deep as it had during the fall of 1986.

The failed drug test represented the start of Gooden's public saga with drugs. He would suffer several relapses, tainting a career that had begun with such promise. For Mets broadcaster Howie Rose, Gooden's drug problems rank as the biggest controversy he's seen during his days as a follower of the Mets.

"I think clearly Dwight Gooden's drug involvements were the biggest stories that impacted the team apart from things that happened on the field," says Rose with some degree of sadness. "That first day that he announced that he would be going into rehab was such a stunner, not so much in light of his recent behavior leading up to that, but just because of what he appeared to be those first two years [in the major leagues]. Even though his

Unleashing a pitch with his classic over-the-top delivery, Dwight Gooden displays vintage form. Rich Pilling/MLB Photos/Getty Images

third year, 1986, they won the World Series, he had lost a bit of his dominance. Not that anybody could have duplicated what he did the year before. But there were a couple of little things that had happened along the way that took a little bit of shine off the image. Still, I don't think anybody really expected to hear what they heard that April morning when it was announced that he was going into rehab."

Gooden's fall from grace emerged as a larger story than even the considerable drug problems of another celebrated teammate.

"I think the continuing story of Gooden was the biggest [controversy], even more so than that of Darryl Strawberry," Rose says. "Somehow with Darryl, it was less surprising than it was with 'Doc.' I think we had built Doc up to be a kid, at least in those first couple of years, that appeared to have his head on straight enough that he would avoid those pitfalls. So I think that part of what transpired was connected to the fact that we never expected—or didn't really expect right away—that he would be one to fall prey to it."

One More Try for "The Franchise"

With drug abuse and injuries laying waste to their starting rotation in 1987, the Mets decided to dip into their storied past for some help. In early June, the Mets offered a tryout to Tom Seaver, who had seemingly retired after ending the 1986 season on the disabled list with the Boston Red Sox. (The injury prevented an enticing matchup of Seaver against the Mets in the World Series). Seaver worked out for 16 days with the Mets, throwing both on the side and in simulated games. Such simulated games usually provide favorable results for major league pitchers, but Seaver pitched poorly—no match for even minor league hitters. On June 22, Seaver officially announced his retirement, ending his third stint with the Mets before it really even began. He didn't make it to the 25-man roster, opting to call it quits rather than embarrass himself in the Mets uniform he had worn with such class and talent.

The 30-30 Club

Although the 1987 season ended in disappointment—a second-place finish to the seemingly less talented St. Louis Cardinals—the Mets did achieve an unprecedented offensive milestone. Both Howard Johnson and Darryl Strawberry joined the 30-30 club, each hitting at least 30 home runs while stealing 30 bases, marking the first time in history that teammates had achieved 30-30 in the same season.

Johnson's performance was particularly eye-popping. After the Mets failed to re-sign popular third baseman Ray Knight during the winter, Johnson faced immediate pressure from angry fans who couldn't help but make comparisons. Well, by the end of the season, it was clear that Johnson—and not Knight—had emerged as the more talented and more productive player of the two. As the Mets' new starting third baseman and occasional fill-in at shortstop, "HoJo" also became the first National League infielder to attain the 30-30 plateau in a season.

A Disaster of a Deal

If we were to identify a watershed moment that marked the decline of the Mets of the late 1980s, we might begin with the date of June 18, 1989. That's the day that the Mets organization

Darryl Strawberry—an abundance of speed, size, and power—only to be sidetracked by recurring problems with drugs.
Scott Halleran/Getty Images

made one of its largest trades of the decade. With the Mets playing mediocre baseball and their offensive attack mired in fits and starts, the front office decided to make a bold move, sending center fielder Lenny Dykstra and relief pitcher Roger McDowell to the Philadelphia Phillies for infielder-outfielder Juan Samuel.

Intrigued by his combination of power and speed, the Mets felt that Samuel could jump start the offense while also making a successful transition from second base to center field. Unfortunately, neither happened. Though always ill suited to play the infield, Samuel floundered just as much in center field, where he lacked the quick jump and range of Dykstra. Samuel also struggled at the plate, striking out too much and swinging at too many breaking pitches out of the strike zone.

The Mets never recovered from the deal with the Phillies. Samuel not only became a misfit in New York, but the team also came to miss Dykstra's skill as a leadoff man, and the workman-like abilities of McDowell in the bullpen. In addition, team chemistry suffered some damage. Dykstra's departure removed some much-needed aggressiveness and zeal, while the removal of McDowell left many teammates pining for his tension-easing clubhouse pranks and raucous sense of humor.

Some observers have argued that the Mets had already begun to decline as a team, even before the trade with the Phillies. That might be true. If it is, then perhaps the losses of Dykstra and McDowell simply removed any hopes of a Met recovery that might have resulted in a return to their 1986 glory.

McDowell and Myers

The Mets bullpen of the late 1980s provided a ready source for some of the most colorful characters in the history of the franchise. Much of the humor in the Mets clubhouse emanated from

Roger McDowell, the team's part-time closer and full-time prankster.

"Roger was obviously into the whole gamut of different practical jokes and giving hot foots, or hot feet, whatever the proper way to put it is," says Mets broadcaster Howie Rose, who hosted the *Mets Extra* show on WFAN Radio during the McDowell years. "He kept you loose, like Tug McGraw [in an earlier era]. I think McDowell and McGraw were almost clones of each other, McGraw being a left-handed McDowell, and McDowell a right-handed McGraw."

Yet, neither McDowell nor McGraw was the most offbeat character to patrol the Mets bullpen. That honor belongs to another Mets reliever of the late 1980s.

"To me, Randy Myers was probably goofier than both McDowell and McGraw," Rose says. "I mean, Randy Myers, he was into wearing all kinds of military paraphernalia—he was different."

Myers also became linked to a controversial episode that involved unpopular Mets phenom Gregg Jefferies, who had criticized veteran Mets players for failing to care enough about winning. "I remember that incident," says Rose, "where somebody had written on the lineup card in the clubhouse the words 'Do we care?' next to Jefferies's name; it became a big thing. A half a dozen different players, at least within the media, were accused or suspected of having done it. And Myers was one. I remember doing an interview with Randy where I must have asked him a dozen different ways in a five-minute interview, 'Did you do it? Did you do it? Were you the guy?' And he would say things like, 'You know, I'm not the kind of guy who would do that.' He found six different ways to deny six different renditions of the same question. No sooner did I turn the tape recorder off that he looked at me square in the eye and said, 'Yeah, I did it!'"

CHAPTER SEVEN

The 1990s

Failures and Flops

The 1990s turned into the decade of disappointment for the Mets. Expected to contend during the early years of the decade, the Mets watched each season disintegrate into a morass filled with injuries, aging players, and unexpected failures. Given the decade's various calamities, it's no surprise that several key players experienced unforeseen downfalls after showing hints of stardom. As Steve Treder of *The Hardball Times* points out, two players in particular flopped badly—beyond all reasonable expectations:

Carlos Baerga: "The Mets traded the young Jeff Kent for Baerga in mid-1996, just in time to bear the brunt of Baerga's colossal flop," Treder says. At the time of his acquisition, Baerga seemed to be on a collision course with Cooperstown. Playing at a Hall of Fame level his first six seasons, Baerga suddenly fell off the mountaintop in 1996, the same year that the Mets acquired him. Analysts have speculated on the cause of his early downfall, with reasons ranging from a lack of conditioning to an infatuation with a fast-paced nightlife to questions about his birth certificate. Whatever the reason, he never played like a Hall of Famer with the Mets, and his career continued to spiral downward after he left New York in 1998, and he completed the transition from elite All-Star to baseball vagabond.

Butch Huskey: "He looked like a possible emerging star with the Mets in 1997 at the age of 25," recalls Treder. "Four teams later, he was gone from the majors after the 2000 season." Like Baerga, Huskey had problems controlling his weight. Still, it's hard to believe that he played his last major league game at the age of 28. Instead of being recalled as the star power hitter he might have become, Huskey will mostly be remembered as the answer to the following trivia question: "Who was the first designated hitter for the Mets in the regular season?" It was Huskey, on June 16, 1997.

Mental Blocks

Mackey Sasser never flashed the stardom of a Carlos Baerga or Butch Huskey, but he appeared to give the Mets a commodity that they hadn't owned in years: a strong left-handed hitting catcher. (As veteran Kansas City talk show host Danny Clinkscale once said, "Finding a good, left-handed hitting catcher is like finding the Rosetta Stone.") A talented hitter with a strong throwing arm and a lyrical name, the former Mets catcher found himself unable to return the ball back to the pitcher off and on for several years during the late 1980s and early 1990s. The phobia apparently originated in the minor leagues when Sasser hurt his shoulder, causing him to develop bad habits when returning the ball to the mound.

By 1991, Sasser's problem became so acute that he lost his starting catching position with the Mets. Sasser would pound the ball into his mitt repeatedly and then lift and pump his arm, sometimes three or four times, before weakly lobbing the ball back to the pitcher. The Mets decided to try Sasser in the outfield in an effort to make him a utility man, but then cut him loose after the 1992 season. He signed on with the Mariners, but continued to struggle. With his defensive game deteriorating, Sasser also seemed to lose his batting stroke and saw his career come to an end in 1995.

Seaver Enters The Hall

In 1992, Tom Seaver achieved the game's most prestigious individual honor when he earned election and induction to baseball's Hall of Fame. He also received the highest percentage of the balloting in Hall of Fame election history, with votes on just over 98 percent of ballots cast. (Only five writers failed to cast a vote for Seaver.) Seaver officially entered the Hall on August 2, with the small village of Cooperstown providing the backdrop.

"The Hall of Fame was an experience. ... " says Seaver, his voice trailing off. "It's not just everyday stuff; it's forever. You're there forever. It's your whole life in one moment."

For Mets fans and followers, the news of Seaver's election to the Hall of Fame carried a special meaning. Seaver would become the first player to enter the Hall as a Met, with the team's "NY" logo prominently featured on his bronze Hall of Fame plaque. For at least one member of the New York media, the news of Seaver's election created a most memorable evening at work.

"The most memorable night that I spent as a talk show host at WFAN, which is something I did for eight years, was an hour that I spent on the air with Tom the night after he was elected to the Baseball Hall of Fame," says Mets broadcaster Howie Rose. "I built an entire five-hour show around Seaver's career by bringing in guests who had played with him, or in some cases against him. People who had been important parts of his career. And he was the centerpiece. We had him on for an hour; it was only supposed to be a half-hour. It just kept going, and he was more than gracious to double the amount of time he could spend with us. It was just a phenomenal night."

Buckner Surpasses Seaver

Just how significant to baseball history was the Mookie Wilson groundball that sneaked past Bill Buckner in Game 6 of the 1986 World Series? On August 4, 1992, the ball that eluded Buckner's grasp was offered up for bidding in a Manhattan auction. Noted actor Charlie Sheen, a rabid baseball fan and a star in the films *Major League* and *Eight Men Out*, placed the highest bid at $85,000. In contrast, an actual uniform jersey worn by the legendary Tom Seaver, who had been inducted into the Hall of Fame only two days earlier, drew a bid of only $50,000—or $35,000 less than the Wilson-Buckner ball.

The All-Nickname Team

Now that politically correct values and habits have become entrenched in the new millennium, there seems little hope that nicknames will once again become fashionable in baseball. In past eras, nicknames succeeded in making players more colorful to fans, helping the fans to learn more about the players, even at the expense of offending someone who had been given an unwanted nickname.

Although the Mets have existed for a relatively brief time within the context of major league history, the team has succeeded in producing some of the most creative and colorful nicknames of the game's expansion era. With that in mind, let's present the Mets' all-nickname team, position by position:

The Mets' All-Nickname Team

Position	Player	Nickname	Reason
Catcher	Gary Carter	"The Kid"	his boyish enthusiasm
Catcher	Greg Goosen	"The Goose"	a play on his last name
First Base	Donn Clendenon	"Big Train"	his running ability in football
First Base	Keith Hernandez	"Mex"	his Latino heritage
Second Base	Felix Millan	"The Cat"	in homage to cartoon character "Felix The Cat" and Millan's quickness
Shortstop	Frank Taveras	"Man of Steal"	his base-stealing ability
Third Base	Wayne Garrett	"Red"	the color of his hair
Left Field	John Milner	"The Hammer"	his similarity to Hank Aaron, a.k.a "The Hammer"
Center Field	Lenny Dykstra	"Nails"	his rugged, hard-nosed style of play
Right Field	George Theodore	"The Stork"	his tall, awkward build
DH (imaginary)	Dave Kingman	"King Kong"	his gorilla-like strength
Starting Pitcher	Tom Seaver	"The Franchise"	his superstar worth to the team
		"Tom Terrific"	in tribute to his greatness
Relief Pitcher	Danny Frisella	"Bear"	his rugged frame
Relief Pitcher	Tom Hall	"The Blade"	his thin, wispy build

Firecrackers and Bleach

The Mets may have reached the low point of the franchise's existence during the 1993 season. In late July, two ugly incidents involving Mets players took place within the span of one week. On July 24, outfielder Vince Coleman decided to welcome some autograph seekers by throwing a live firecracker at them in the parking lot of Dodger Stadium. Three fans—including a one-year-old baby, an 11-year-old child, and a 33-year-old woman— suffered minor injuries from the incident. In response, the fans filed felony charges against Coleman, who claimed that he had thrown the firecracker as merely a prank. And then, three days after the Coleman incident, pitcher Bret Saberhagen filled a water gun with bleach and sprayed several reporters with the toxic substance. Saberhagen offered an explanation similarly bizarre to Coleman's claims, rationalizing that he intended to spray some members of the Mets front office instead of the reporters. Ah, as if spraying the front office people would have been more acceptable.

Dallas Green

Not much went right during Dallas Green's tenure as Mets manager. Expected to restore law and order to an anti-social club-house, Green succeeded only in alienating most of his players. The methods of discipline that Green had skillfully used in guiding the 1980 Phillies to the world championship no longer seemed to work with the less tolerant players of the 1990s. Green also drew criticism from some for his handling of the Mets' three top pitching prospects—Paul Wilson, Bill Pulsipher, and Jason Isringhausen—collectively known as "Generation K." With some critics claiming that the manager hurt each of their youthful arms through misuse, Green fared no better in leading the Mets than his failed predecessor, Jeff Torborg.

Fortunately for Green, his most lasting legacy as Mets manager might involve his relatively little-known membership in an exclusive club. He is one of only four men to manage both the Mets and the Yankees. The others are Casey Stengel, Yogi Berra, and Joe Torre, all of whom are either in the Hall of Fame or destined for future enshrinement.

Gender-Bending

As the strike by the Major League Baseball Players' Association lingered into the spring of 1995, the Mets made efforts to field a team of replacement players. Not satisfied with the usual pool of candidates (former major leaguers, career minor leaguers, or rank amateurs), the Mets offered tryouts to two *women*. Infielder Shannan Mitchem and pitcher Ann Williams, stars with the all-female Colorado Silver Bullets professional franchise, reported to the Mets' spring training base in Port St. Lucie, Florida.

The tryouts of Mitchem and Williams didn't last long. Both players were given their releases—after one day.

The Man with the Helmet

On December 20, 1996, general manager Joe McIlvaine made one of the best trades of his regime. Unafraid to deal young talent for older, proven commodities, McIlvaine acquired 1993 American League batting champion John Olerud from the Toronto Blue Jays for young right-hander Robert Person. Olerud not only provided the Mets with their best first base play since the heyday of Keith Hernandez, but also garnered some attention for his choice of headwear while playing first base. Of all the major leaguers in the 1990s, Olerud was the only one to regularly wear a batting helmet at his position in the field, excluding those ever-endangered members of the catching fraternity. Olerud's choice of headgear stemmed from a near tragic incident he endured during his college years; while attending Washington State University in 1989, Olerud suffered a brain hemorrhage and an aneurysm during a morning workout. Though he recovered, doctors advised him to wear a protective batting helmet while playing first base or pitching (he was a two-position player in college), in order to protect against line drives and collisions with base runners that might result in contact with the skull.

By now it would probably be safe for Olerud to discard the helmet in favor of a soft cap, but matters of habit and superstition have compelled him to continue wearing the hard hat at all times throughout his professional career. While he remains the lone active major leaguer to wear a helmet in the field—Olerud finished out the 2004 season with the Yankees—he is by no means the first to do so in the post-World War II history of the game. It's happened from time to time over the past 50 years, dating back to the first team that made full-temple helmets a permanent addition to their inventory of baseball equipment. During the 1953 season, the Pittsburgh Pirates became the first team to permanently adopt batting helmets, taking the field wearing rather primitive fiberglass "miner's caps" at the mandate of general manager Branch Rickey, who also owned stock in the company producing the helmets.

Twins in the Pen

The bullpen has long been a place for hijinks and humor, largely because it is located far away from the disciplinary eye of a team's manager. As a result, the occurrences that take place in the bullpen are often allowed to reach proportions of immaturity that would not be tolerated elsewhere. But even the bullpen has its limits, as the Mets discovered in 1997.

As general manager Steve Phillips watched the Mets play the Expos at Shea Stadium on September 13, he noticed reliever Corey Lidle sitting in the bullpen. Although there was nothing strange about that, Phillips also noticed that the player sitting next to Lidle looked just like Lidle. For a moment, Phillips might have thought that he was looking at Lidle's evil doppelganger, but he soon realized that the Lidle lookalike was none other than Lidle's twin brother, Kevin. And that didn't sit well with Phillips.

Although Kevin Lidle was dressed in a Mets uniform, he was not a part of the team or the organization in any way. Worse than that, Lidle played for another team; he was actually a minor league catcher with the Detroit Tigers organization, which was on the verge of releasing him. Either way, Phillips was furious that a non-Met was sitting in the home bullpen at Shea Stadium. Phillips angrily called the bullpen, ordering that Kevin Lidle be removed from the premises immediately.

It's safe to say that Kevin Lidle never made another appearance in the Mets' bullpen. As a matter of fact, he's never appeared in a major league game either.

Valentine's Day

It remains one of the most bizarre episodes in franchise history—and literally ranks as a *Tale from the Dugout*. After being ejected from a game in June of 1999, Mets manager Bobby Valentine decided to sneak back into the Shea Stadium dugout wearing a disguise that was more comical than concealing. Donning a fake mustache made out of black eye stickers and wearing a pair of sunglasses, Valentine took his illegal place near the dugout exit that led to the clubhouse. From there, he continued to manage the game for the Mets.

Cameras soon caught Valentine on video. While much of the reaction from the sports media was more amused than it was outraged, the National League office saw little humor in the incident. Two days after Valentine's theatrics, the league handed him a two-game suspension and a $5,000 fine.

Wild-Card Collapse

In late September of 1999, the Mets opened up a seemingly comfortable four-game lead over the Cincinnati Reds for the National League's wild-card spot. With only 10 days remaining in the regular season, the identity of the final playoff team in the NL seemed certain. Or maybe not.

The Mets suddenly went into a freefall, losing seven straight games while playing some of their worst ball of the season. The losing streak spurred rumors that the Mets might actually fire Bobby Valentine *before* the end of the season, a circumstance practically unheard of in baseball annals. Who would the Mets have turned to? Perhaps one of their coaches, such as Cookie Rojas? Or first base coach Mookie Wilson? Or how about a past manager like Dallas Green? Well, let's not get ridiculous. Then, just as the Mets reached the depths of what some were calling the greatest collapse since the 1964 Phillies, the team rebounded, with Valentine remaining in charge. After sweeping the final three regularly scheduled games against the Pirates, the desperate

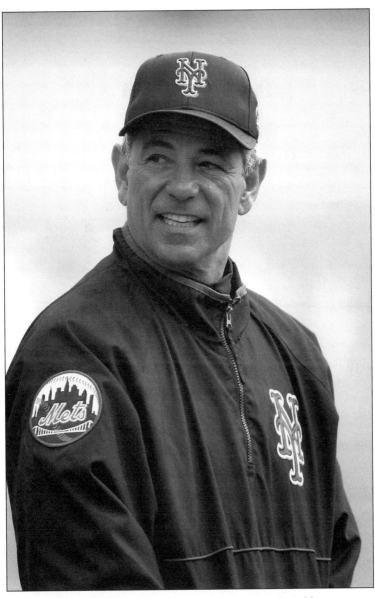

Often brilliant, sometimes bizarre and unconventional, Bobby Valentine frequently made headlines in leading the Mets to two postseason berths. Eliot Schechter/Getty Images

Mets clinched a wild-card tie with the Reds. That set the stage for the first tie-breaking playoff game in Mets history.

Breaking the Tie

Circumstances favored the Mets in their 1999 playoff tiebreaker. The Reds were exhausted, having waited out a 347-minute rain delay in their final regularly scheduled game against the Milwaukee Brewers. More importantly, the pitching match up tilted heavily in the direction of New York. The Mets confidently handed the ball to their left-handed ace, Al Leiter, set to pitch on his usual four days' rest. In contrast, the latest turn in Cincinnati's starting rotation fell upon journeyman Steve Parris. Although Parris had surprised some observers by winning 11 of 14 decisions during the summer, his pedigree lacked the impressiveness of Leiter. A veteran of postseason play, Leiter had started the seventh game of the 1997 World Series for the world champion Florida Marlins.

Playing in front of a capacity crowd at Cincinnati's Cinergy Field, the Mets took advantage of Parris from the opening pitch. After Rickey Henderson reached on a leadoff single, Edgardo Alfonzo clubbed Parris's sixth pitch of the night over the left-field wall. The Mets then added single runs in the third, fifth, and sixth innings, including a solo home run by Henderson.

The ample run support proved more than sufficient for a masterful Leiter, who pitched his finest game of the season. He allowed only two hits in shutting down one of the league's most potent offensive lineups. When Dmitri Young hit Leiter's 133rd pitch right to Alfonzo at second base, the left-hander's night—and the playoff tiebreaker—came to an end. The Mets poured onto the field to celebrate a 5-0 shutout and the franchise's first trip to the postseason since 1988. The decade-long drought had finally come to an end.

CHAPTER EIGHT

2000 and Beyond

The Hammer

The cancer-related death of former major league slugger John Milner in the year 2000 barely rated a mention in several of the New York City newspapers. Sadly, much of the New York media had forgotten the promise and popularity of Milner, who at one time seemed destined to become the franchise's first great homegrown home run hitter. Milner's powerful swing reminded some observers of a left-handed version of Hank Aaron, earning him the same nickname as Aaron, "The Hammer." Although Milner never fulfilled the potential stardom that some had forecast for him, he was just about the best position player the Mets had during their lean years in the mid-1970s. He was popular with fans, many of whom fell in love with his smooth, left-handed swing and tape-measure home runs. Milner also came from an era when real nicknames were still in vogue and made the players more colorful and endearing to the average fan. So long, Hammer.

John Milner didn't live up to star billing in his days as a Met, but his long home runs made him a popular figure at Shea Stadium.
Focus on Sport/Getty Images

Hendu

During the 2000 season, the Mets wanted to give Rickey Henderson every chance to redeem himself after a series of disciplinary transgressions. They had hoped that he might embark on a hot streak and build up the trade value that he had managed to eradicate through an early season of lackadaisical play. The Mets were prepared to give Henderson that chance, but two more incidents convinced the Mets that it was finally time to cut their losses.

In a Friday night game against the Florida Marlins, Henderson rifled a shot deep toward left field. Assuming that the ball would clear the left-field wall, Henderson went into one of baseball's recently developed bad habits—the premature home-run trot. By the time the ball was retrieved and thrown to the infield, Henderson could advance no farther than first base, even though he should have easily reached second with a double. After the game, Henderson refused to apologize for his lack of hustle. In fact, he told reporters that he would do it again! In other words, he was sending the message that a showy home-run trot had become more important than advancing as many bases as possible. And this from the all-time stolen base king!

The next day, Henderson confronted a reporter for the *New York Post* who had dared to criticize him for his base running faux pas the previous night. In the course of their exchange, Henderson made an indirect threat toward the reporter. When general manager Steve Phillips learned about the latest incident, he felt that the time had come to end what had become an embarrassing and distracting circus. Phillips gave Henderson his release that day, ending his brief but stormy tenure with the team.

The sad thing about the Henderson saga is that the Mets and their fans, who were basically innocent bystanders all along, came out on the short end. The Mets had to pay the balance of Hendu's $2 million salary in 2000, while the fans at Shea Stadium were deprived of watching an extraordinary leadoff man—at least when he wanted to be. As for Henderson, he received full pay without any suspension or fine, and was permitted the freedom to pick his new team. Sometimes, there is no justice.

Aging Not So Gracefully

What's the difference between a 21-year-old and a 26-year-old? In the world of baseball prospects, just about everything. When the Mets sent hard-throwing right-hander Lesli Brea to Baltimore as part of the return package for shortstop Mike Bordick during the summer of 2000, the Orioles thought they were acquiring a young man who had barely reached the legal drinking age, a youngster who they could bring along slowly over the next two seasons. Then, some Baltimore writers noticed a photo of Brea in the Mets' media guide and began speculating that the Orioles' new prospect looked like he was closer to 30 than he was to 20. Finally, a reporter asked Brea how old he was. "Twenty-six," responded Brea, who had suddenly picked up five years of time on this earth. The pronouncement certainly came as disturbing news to the Orioles, especially considering that Brea had not managed a promotion past Single-A during the first four years of his minor league career with the Mets.

Terminology

Prior to the 2000 World Series between the Mets and the Yankees, baseball historians and researchers believed that the term "Subway Series" had originated in a Willard Mullin cartoon that appeared in 1941. As it turns out, the findings of researcher Barry Popik shows that the term is at least five years older than that. The phrase "Subway Series" actually appears to have originated in 1936, when the New York Giants played the Yankees in that year's World Series. On September 17, 1936, two publications—the *New York World-Telegram* and *The Sporting News*—used the term Subway Series in headlines. A few days later, the *New York Post* followed the lead of the other publications and also referred to a Subway Series.

Although these are the earliest references we know of, it's important to remember that research is continuing in this area. It's possible that there exist earlier references to Subway Series that have yet to be discovered.

Blunders on the Base Paths

It has become baseball's bad habit, and it finally reached its valley of embarrassment in Game 1 of the 2000 World Series. On three different occasions, Mets base runners failed to run hard on batted balls, costing them a minimum of two at-bats and at least one run. And despite Bobby Valentine's protestations to the contrary, shoddy base running ranked as the number-one reason the Mets lost Game 1—plain and simple.

For too many years now, it's become fashionable among some major league players not to run out batted balls—whether they be routine grounders, high pop-ups, or long drives that the batter *thinks* will be a home run. Somehow, it's become the "in thing" to pause and preen instead, either to admire one's own home run handiwork or to look "cool" by casually strutting down the first base line. Whatever the reasons for the lack of hustle, the nonsense on the base paths needs to come to a stop.

In the case of the Mets during Game 1 of the Series, Todd Zeile added the "assumption of a foul ball" to the growing list of base running transgressions. After topping a weak roller down the third base line, Zeile assumed that the ball would stay foul, even though it was close to the line and had a funny sidespin to it. Once Scott Brosius noticed that Zeile had essentially taken the play for granted, he smartly waited for the ball to roll back into fair territory, calmly picked it up, and threw to first for an easy 5-3 putout. If Zeile had run hard from the moment he had hit the ball, Brosius likely would have picked up the ball before it slid back into fair territory, not wanting to test the fates on a close play at first base. And who knows what Zeile might have done with a prolonged at-bat.

A lack of understanding the rules also appeared to contribute to the Mets' follies on the base paths. When Jay Payton topped a ball near home plate, it first bounced behind the plate before caroming into fair territory, where Jorge Posada fielded it and completed the rarely seen 2-2 putout. Although Payton might have thought the ball had bounced off of Posada in foul territory (thus making it a dead ball), it appeared that he was under the impression that once the ball bounced behind the plate, it was automatically and immediately foul. In fairness to Payton, Posada probably would have been able to throw him out easily at first base if he had run hard from the start, but then again, who knows for sure? If Payton had forced Posada to make a throw, perhaps the Yankees catcher would have thrown the ball in the dirt or past Tino Martinez down the right field line. By making the wrong assumption (for whatever reason he did), Payton gift-wrapped an easy out for Posada, rather than challenge him to make a tougher play.

Yet, the errors of Payton and Zeile paled in comparison to a critical base-running blunder by Timoniel "Timo" Perez in the sixth inning. Running from first base on Zeile's long drive to left field, Perez slowed down near second base and began the celebratory pumping of his first in the air, thinking that the ball would land in the left-field stands. When the ball hit the absolute top of the padded wall in left and bounced back into the field of play, Perez started running hard again. By the time he reached home plate, Posada already had the ball in his glove, allowing him to apply the tag to the late-arriving Perez. Instead of owning a 1-0 lead with another runner in scoring position, the Mets found themselves still embedded in a scoreless deadlock and lost the opportunity to bring another batter to the plate. (By the way, Zeile wasn't blameless here, either; he too assumed the ball had achieved home-run distance and stopped running hard between first and second.) The Mets would come to rue the loss of a sure-fire run later in the game, when the Yankees tied the game in the bottom of the ninth and then won it on Jose Vizcaino's single in the 12th.

Misplay at the Plate

Virtually no analysts on television or in print saw fit to discuss it, but the Mets' Mike Piazza badly misplayed Jay Payton's fine throw on Luis Sojo's World Series-clinching hit in Game 5. As a rule, a catcher should do everything in his power to prevent a ball from hitting an oncoming runner; otherwise he has no chance of making a tag play. For some reason, Piazza set up on the foul side of the third base line, thus allowing Payton's throw to hit Jorge Posada and carom into the dugout, which enabled the Yankees to bring home a second run on the play. Piazza should have taken a position slightly toward the fair side of the third base line, while straddling the line with his left foot. That way, he would have been sure to catch the ball, and by using his left foot to hold up the runner, still might have had a chance to tag Posada. At the very least, Piazza would have been able to corral the throw, preventing the Yankees from scoring a second run. The Mets then could have approached the bottom of the ninth by trying to manufacture a run, rather than try to get someone on base and hope for a home run against Mariano Rivera, always an unlikely occurrence.

Tommie Agee

Most days in January don't produce much baseball news, except for a late-winter free agent signing or the sad reporting of the death of a former player. The latter occurrence struck the Mets organization on January 22, 2001, resulting in one of the sadder days in franchise history. Few Mets achieved a higher state of popularity than Tommie Agee, who succumbed to a massive heart attack that day while leaving his New York City office. Agee was only 58, which made the news all the more unbearable. Although Agee played only a handful of his 12 seasons with the Mets and didn't start or finish his career with the franchise, he became a lasting symbol of the team's unexpected success in 1969. Displaying his vintage Gold Glove defense against the Baltimore Orioles, Agee made two acrobatic catches for the Mets in Game 3 of the 1969 World Series. The pair of catches helped the Mets win the game and a take a two games-to-one lead in the Series. And let's not forget what Agee did during the regular season in 1969, when he hit a career-high 26 home runs as the team's everyday center fielder. That year Agee also belted the only upper-deck home run in Shea Stadium history. His April 10 blastoff against Montreal's Larry Jaster is still commemorated with Agee's number "20" on the seat.

A Tribute

At one time, right-hander Pat Strange was one of the Mets' top pitching prospects, but he never achieved the expected level of success because of a serious injury to his elbow. Still, Strange deserves to be part of the Mets legacy because of a noble gesture he made after the 2002 season. Pat and his wife named their newborn son Brian Cole Strange, in memory of a former Mets prospect who was killed in a car accident during the spring of 2001. Twenty two-year-old Brian Cole, a talented outfielder with speed and power and a onetime teammate of Strange, was one of the most highly regarded youngsters in the Mets organization. In the year 2000, Cole batted a combined .301 with 19 home runs and 86 RBIs for the Mets affiliates at St. Lucie (Class-A) and Binghamton (Class-AA). If Cole had lived, he might have eventually filled a role as the team's leadoff hitter, a position that became such a trouble spot for the Mets after their National League championship season of 2000.

Orange Alert

In the spring of 2003, the Mets unveiled bright orange jerseys—with decidedly awful armpit stripes. Some observers, including this author, branded the uniforms as simply horrid, worse even than the all-red pajamas used by the 1975 Cleveland Indians and those bright red/orange uniforms sported by the Baltimore Orioles in 1971. Even actress Sigourney Weaver, who was asked to model one of the new shirts at the start of spring training, didn't look that good showcasing the new look. Thank goodness the Mets opted not to wear their new "Orange Alert" uniforms in regular-season games. After donning them in pregame warmups, the Mets removed the orange jerseys in favor of their usual white or black shirt colors.

No Comparison to Clemente

There's no such thing as a "can't-miss" prospect in baseball, where many a first-round draft choice never even make the major leagues. Still, the Mets were thrilled to take fleet-footed and highly touted high school outfielder Lastings Milledge of Bradenton, Florida, with their first pick in the 2003 amateur draft. Mets scouts raved about his defensive skills, specifically his ability to read the ball off the bat and gain a quick jump on fly balls and line drives. Now it's one thing for scouts to offer assessments of players, but it's quite another when agents become involved in the business of player evaluation. One player agent dared to compare Milledge's defensive abilities favorably with those of Hall of Famer Roberto Clemente. Of course, that particular comparison needed to be taken with an extra grain of salt, given that it came from Milledge's own agent, Tommy Tanzer. Thankfully, Tanzer restored some semblance of truth to his evaluation when he admitted that his client "doesn't have the arm that Roberto had." Of course, no right fielder in the history of the game has ever combined the arm strength and accuracy of the Pittsburgh Pirates' superstar, who was fittingly dubbed "The Great One."

Milledge had recently concluded his scholastic career at Lakewood Ranch High School, where he played for former major league outfielder Dave Moates, who played for the Rangers in the 1970s. A high school coach for over 20 years, Moates has overseen the development of several future major leaguers at Lakewood Ranch, including the Tampa Bay Devil Rays' Lance Carter and the Padres' Brian Tolberg.

Big Mo

At one time, Mo Vaughn played a decent first base, but those days seemed like, and indeed were, so last century given his performance in 2003. With apologies to Zeke Bonura, Dave "King Kong" Kingman, and Dick "Dr. Strangeglove" Stuart, Vaughn just might have been the worst defensive first baseman in major league history, at least based on his performance in the 2002 and 2003 seasons.

Combining Bonura's statuesque mobility with Stuart's bad hands, Vaughn became such a huge defensive liability that he affected the confidence level of other infielders when making even routine throws to first base. And then there's the matter of Vaughn's conditioning. (As one Mets fan told me, "It looks like Vaughn gains weight *during* the game. I swear he looks 10 pounds heavier at the end of nine innings than he did at the start.") For all the talk of Vaughn having reported to spring training lighter than the previous season, he still remained about 30 pounds overweight. Sadly, that just made him an easier target for the boo birds at Shea Stadium.

Murph

In the summer of 2004, the Mets lost more than a broadcaster when Bob Murphy succumbed to lung cancer at the age of 79; they lost an integral piece of their history that linked the franchise's inaugural season to the new millennium, stretching from the days of Casey Stengel to the era of Mike Piazza. Murphy was never that highly regarded or fully appreciated when he worked Mets TV broadcasts with Ralph Kiner and Lindsey Nelson. Kiner, with his propensity for malaprops and down-home story-telling, and Nelson with his loud sports coats and frenetically excitable on-air style, tended to dominate the broadcasts. Then, in the early 1980s, the Mets decided to move Murphy over to the radio side fulltime, and that's where he really became the voice of the Mets.

Although Murphy considered the move a demotion of sorts, he truly shined in the radio booth, where the need for explicit descriptions of plays as they happened better fit his broadcasting style. Within a few years, Murphy's brilliant work on the radio had resurrected his career. By the late 1980s and early 1990s, Murphy had developed a whole new following and was no longer the overlooked third man in the booth. Then came the Hall of Fame's Frick Award, much deserved and perhaps overdue, in 1994.

Murphy did such an excellent job of both describing the play-by-play in full detail, while also keeping up with the pace of the action at the same time. You always understood the way a play developed with Murphy at the microphone. He never had to backtrack in describing a play; he almost always got it right the first time around.

One of the hidden aspects of Murphy's broadcasting style was his sense of humor. He didn't use it very often, saving it only for those moments he considered the most appropriate—while sometimes targeting himself as the butt of the jokes. One of Murphy's funniest lines occurred during an interview he did with Billy Sample of MLB Radio in the fall of 2003, just before his retirement. Sample asked him how he would like to be remembered. Offering a simple deadpan response, Murphy said, "Favorably."

He will be.

Living a Broadcaster's Dream

For a lifelong Mets fan like Gary Cohen, working with Bob Murphy on Mets radio broadcasts from 1989 through 2003 represented one of the peaks of his journalistic career. "I grew up in New York. I had listened to Murph from the time I was six years old, and was a huge Mets fan growing up," says Cohen, one of the best play-by-play men in the major leagues. "I was very fortunate to have been offered the chance to work for the Mets and do their radio broadcasts. I don't think that there was a time over the course of 15 years working with Murph that I didn't pinch myself that here I was sitting next to this incredible legendary broadcaster who I had grown up listening to."

Spending his boyhood days as a fan who listened to Murphy helped give Cohen some early insights how to perform a good, professional broadcast. Yet, the experience also set up a subconscious obstacle for Cohen, one that he needed to work hard to overcome.

"I had listened to Murph for so long that I noticed when I came back to New York and began working for the Mets that a lot of Murph had seeped into me," Cohen says. "Without even being conscious of it, just from having listened to so many games over the years, a lot of the mechanics and a lot of the descriptions that Murph used, I found that I was using, too. I actually had to wean myself away from that because working alongside him, it would have been a little bit odd to use similar phrasings."

With that trap avoided, Cohen and Murphy established themselves as one of the smoothest, most articulate broadcast teams in the sport. They transformed Mets games into a near work of art, making the radio broadcasts enjoyable even for those who had little interest in who won or lost.

Learning from the Master

Bob Murphy's talent with words pleased Mets fans for decades, but it was his enthusiasm and work ethic that taught Gary Cohen and other young announcers some important lessons about broadcasting.

"Murph [set] a great example," says Cohen. "What I learned from Murph, well there were two things. First, *every game is important.* Murph had this wonderful ability to make every game special, whether it was a game between two last-place teams in the middle of August or whether it was Game 7 in the World Series.

"The other thing was, from the day he started until the day he retired, he never mailed it in. He worked hard every day, he showed up early. He made sure that he was prepared fully for every broadcast and never relied on just his laurels and who he was. He always felt that he owed it to the listeners to work as he hard as he could, and bring his A-game, and he did."

Kiner's Korner

The passing of the beloved Bob Murphy left Ralph Kiner as the sole surviving member of the Mets' original broadcast team. To more recent generations of fans, Kiner has become far better known as a broadcaster than as a player—even though he was a Hall of Fame slugger—in part because of the passage of time but also because of his storytelling abilities and some unusual tendencies in the broadcast booth. Other than longtime San Diego Padres broadcaster Jerry Coleman, no baseball announcer is more associated with the malaprops than Mr. Kiner. Here are just a few collected during Kiner's 40-plus years as a broadcaster:

On the Mets' ability to play well on the road:

"All of the Mets' road wins against the Dodgers this year occurred at Dodger Stadium."

Describing a recent spate of poor play by the Mets:

"If Casey Stengel were alive today, he'd be spinning in his grave."

Describing the supposed adventures of a Mets base runner:

"Kevin McReynolds stops at third, and he scores.

Introducing the Mets' next scheduled batter, Gary Carter:

"Now up to bat for the Mets is Gary Cooper."

Offering an irrefutable baseball truth:

"Solo homers usually come with no one on base."

Promoting Induction Weekend at the National Baseball Hall of Fame and Museum:

"The Hall of Fame ceremonies are on the 31st and 32nd of July."

Providing a bit of circular logic:

"The reason the Mets have played so well at Shea this year is they have the best home record in baseball."

Discussing the passing of talent from one generation to another:

"There's a lot of heredity in that family."

One day, while making perhaps his most memorable introduction on *Kiner's Korner*:

"Hello, everybody. Welcome to 'Kiner's Korner.' This is ... uh. I'm ... uh."

Early Halloween

Toward the end of the 2004 season, the Mets participated in an annual tradition, making their rookies wear unusual costumes on getaway day. After New York's 3-2 victory on a Sunday afternoon against the Cubs, the rookies had to wear the costumes while walking out of the clubhouse, sign autographs for fans, and then play dress-up as they walked through LaGuardia Airport before boarding the team charter to Atlanta. According to the ritual, the rookies would have to maintain their costumed looks until they reached their hotel in Atlanta.

Originally, the rookies were supposed to wear the costumes on the trip home from Montreal on Thursday, so that they would have to pass through customs. Since that game ended so late, the ritual was put off until Sunday.

Third baseman David Wright garnered the most attention for the "Strawberry Tart" outfit that he was forced to wear. It was not a good fit for Wright. The skirt was too short, the leggings too tight, and the wig clearly didn't match the size of his head.

"It's part of the rookie process, but I don't feel too comfortable right now," Wright said, brushing the strawberry locks from his eyes. "The bad news is that I have to go sign autographs now for all the people who were cheering for us before."

Tyler Yates, a native of Hawaii, had to wear a hula girl outfit replete with coconut brassiere.

"I got hosed because I'm from Hawaii," said a frustrated Yates.

Other Mets players were forced to adorn themselves in a variety of costumes, all of which were purchased by team captain John Franco. Bartolome Fortunato dressed as a cow, Craig Brazell as a ladybug, Heath Bell as a nun, Victor Diaz as "Batman," Joe Hietpas as "Superman," and Jose Reyes as a clown. Even Kaz Matsui, a veteran of the Japanese Leagues but a rookie in the major leagues, joined in on the fun by wearing a "Spiderman" outfit. His interpreter, Noz Matsumoto, was also forced into the action, dressing in a "Supergirl" costume that was too small for Reyes. The biggest laugh was accorded to a non-player—massage specialist Yosh Nishio—who was dressed as Elvis Presley, circa his weightier days in 1974.

(Editor's note: Thanks to Maxwell Kates and Ron Bleiberg for providing this story.)

A New Era

When the Mets announced that Willie Randolph would assume their managerial reins after the team's disastrous 2004 season, it hardly seemed newsworthy that he became the first African-American skipper in franchise history. Perhaps it's because so many other black managers have come before Randolph (ever since Frank Robinson's hiring by the Cleveland Indians in 1975), or perhaps because some of us had to stop and think whether the Mets had ever employed a black manager. Even if not particularly newsworthy in the enlightened era of the 2000s, Randolph's hiring certainly does rank as historic. And for those who think that the Mets dawdled in taking over 40 years to bring in a minority manager, consider that the rival Yankees have never had one—at least not through the reign of Joe Torre.

Unfortunately, African-American players aren't often referred to as smart or as overachievers, but Randolph classified as both throughout his playing days. Driven by an endless work ethic and a fierce desire to improve, Randolph showed continual progress as he moved up baseball's developmental ladder. Considered too small by some and too weak a hitter by others, Randolph emerged as a thinking-man's player who displayed patience at the plate, worked the count, hit behind the runners, and carefully measured the deliveries and pickoff moves of opposing pitchers. The end result? Randolph became an excellent table-setting hitter, an accomplished base stealer, and an aggres-

The Mets decided to hire from outside of the organization in naming Willie Randolph their manager after the 2004 season.
Ezra Shaw/Getty Images

sive base runner in addition to flashing superior defensive abilities at second base.

After being acquired from the Pittsburgh Pirates in a blockbuster 1975 deal, Randolph proved a mainstay at second base for the Yankees, remaining there through the end of the 1988 season. Replaced by Steve Sax, Randolph signed a free agent contract with Sax' former team, the Los Angeles Dodgers. He emerged as the Dodgers' MVP in 1989 and then spent his first 26 games of the 1990 season in southern California before being traded to the A's for outfielder Stan Javier. In 1991, Randolph attended the Milwaukee Brewers' spring training camp as a non-roster invitee, worked his way onto the team, and proceeded to bat .327 in 124 games. Surprisingly, the Brewers let him become a free agent, which resulted in his return to New York—this time as a member of the Mets. He batted .252 in 90 games for the Mets before retiring at the end of the 1992 season.

Now fully known for his intelligence and enthusiasm, Randolph moved on to the front office, becoming the Yankees' assistant general manager in 1993. Yet, Randolph felt far more comfortable in uniform; he returned to pinstripes the following season as a coach for manager Buck Showalter and remained in the Bronx through the first nine years of the Torre regime. Like former Yankee coach Chris Chambliss, Randolph interviewed for several major league managerial positions, but didn't receive his first opportunity until agreeing to become the Mets manager during the winter of 2004-2005. It remains in dispute whether he was actually offered the Cincinnati Reds' managerial post at one time; Randolph has insisted he never received an offer, but some members of the Reds organization claim otherwise.

In reacting to Randolph's hiring by the Mets, some members of the New York media criticized the move for perhaps the most ridiculous of reasons, decrying Willie's baseball heritage *as a*

Yankee. That seems more than a bit silly given Randolph's winning pedigree: as a player, he played on two world championship teams, and as a coach, he contributed to four more World Series titlists. Mets fans shouldn't concern themselves with Randolph's ties to the Yankees. They should be far more enthused with his association to winning. (And for those concerned with accuracy, Randolph did play one season for the Mets—his last in the major leagues—giving him at least some previous association with the franchise.)

Bobby Valentine, one of Randolph's predecessors in the Mets' managerial chair, was asked by the *New York Post* to give the new skipper some advice about leading his new team.

"Get his rest, 'cause he's gonna need his energy," Valentine told the *Post* in December of 2004. "[He should] try to learn as much about the organization as possible. And use Yankee references as little as possible."

From a political perspective, Valentine's last suggestion about limiting "Yankee references" would probably win Randolph some public relations points. Yet, if Randolph's many winning experiences in the Bronx somehow rub off on his new team in Queens, most Mets fans will be happy to tolerate the teachings of a former Yankee.

List of Sources

PUBLICATIONS:

The Baseball Chronicle
The Baseball Timeline
The Baseball Encyclopedia
Long Island Press
The New York Mets by Leonard Koppett
New York *Daily News*
New York Post
The New York Times
The Sporting News Official Baseball Guide (1969)
The Sporting News Official Baseball Guide (1970)
The Sporting News Official Baseball Guide (1974)
The Sporting News Official Baseball Guide (1978)
Total Baseball (8th Edition)

WEB SITES:

www.baseball-almanac.com
www.baseballprimer.com
www.baseball-reference.com
www.historicbaseball.com
www.retrosheet.org
www.thehardballtimes.com

Celebrate the Heroes of New York Sports
in These Other Releases from Sports Publishing!